THE THINKING RAT

THE NEW SCIENCE OF ANIMAL LEARNING

OSKAR PINEÑO

ISBN: 1-450-58042-4
ISBN-13: 978-1-450-58042-7

First published: July 2010
www.opineno.com

To Jessica

CONTENTS

PREFACE

For more than a century, animal learning and animal cognition have been (and still are) areas central to research in psychology. Yet, animal psychology remains greatly misunderstood. Among laymen, animal psychologists are too often thought of as animal trainers or pet therapists (or, worse, some sort of animal *whisperers* with obscure abilities to see through the secrets of the animal mind). In academic circles, and even in psychology departments, animal psychologists still retain the fame of mind deniers, scientists stuck in the early radical behaviorism. It would seem that we have done a poor job in projecting a positive and accurate image of our own profession outside the walls of our laboratories.

A few years ago, my wife and I published an opinion article advocating for the communication of our work to the general public[1]. In that article, we asserted that bringing our science closer to the laymen was not just an option, but a duty. At the time that paper was published, different animal laboratories were reporting findings on diverse cognitive abilities of the laboratory rat. These findings were of the kind that even someone with no prior interest in animal psychology could find interesting. In fact, they became the center of attention in mass media and the web for a short while[2]. But, in my opinion, they deserved much more.

This book represents a modest attempt to fulfill my self-imposed duty of conveying my own interest in animal learning and cognition to a general audience, an audience with little or no prior knowledge of this matter, but with avid interest in this subject. More specifically, this book has been written keeping in mind its potential usefulness as a complement for a regular textbook in an

---

[1] Zilski-Pineño and Pineño (2007).

[2] See http://tinyurl.com/ybe7v9e.

animal learning or animal cognition class at an introductory level. Thus, although some familiarity with the basic concepts in the animal learning and cognition literature will certainly help, no expertise is required to understand the ideas presented in this book.

Because in this book I discuss the work of other people, I need to clarify a few things. First, I decided not to report many details that, although of relevance to the scientist, would only complicate the discussion for the lay reader. Those with a deeper interest are invited to read the original works. In fact, it is my hope that some readers will feel compelled to read the original research after reading this book. Second, my discussion of this work might be somewhat biased – an unavoidable consequence of my personal interest in this topic. The authors of the original works might not necessarily endorse all the statements in this book, including those related to their own work. While they are fully responsible for the great experiments and ideas here reported, only I am to blame for any error or misrepresentation of their work in this book.

A number of people have supported me in one way or another during the writing of this book. I would like to thank Jessica Ramos for her review of an early version of this book; and Aaron Blaisdell for his invaluable feedback on the sections discussing his own research.

I am especially indebted to my beloved wife, Jessica Zilski-Pineno, for her extremely detailed review of a draft of this book, which tremendously improved its readability. But, most importantly, I need to thank her for her infinite patience and encouragement. Ever since I first mentioned that I was considering writing this book, she supported my endeavor and constantly renewed my enthusiasm. It is fair to say that, without her, this book would have not been possible. This book is dedicated to her for many good reasons.

~Oskar Pineño

CHAPTER 1: MEET THE RAT

Rats are not precisely what we call "lovely animals". In fact, they are thought to be dirty animals that live surrounded by trash and excrement. Little kittens and puppies are *cute*, little rats are not: say the word *rat* out loud and you are likely to get a reaction of disgust, if not plain fear. Its reputation is so negative that, in the American culture, the word *rat* has made it to the dictionary with mostly bad connotations: being a *rat* means, among other things, being a betrayer, a criminal informant (for the Mafia[1]), or a non-union employer or breaker of union contracts (for unions). In my Spanish culture, being a rat means being a despicable and miser individual. Why such a bad reputation? As is usually the case, there are certain reasons for these cultural meanings. When someone is being called *a fox* (cunning), *a wolf* (loner), *a tiger* (sexually potent), *a lion* (strong and brave), *a snake* (treacherous[2]), *an owl* (wise, serious, most active at night), *a worm* (plainly contemptible), or *an ass* (stupid, rude, mean). As for other animals widely used in the psychology laboratory, their reputations are somewhat mixed: mice are supposed to be shy and quiet, pigeons are dupes, monkeys are mischievous, and apes are uncivilized[3]. In this collection of animals that have a (not always positive) psychological meaning for us, rats are not precisely the winners.

---

[1] A good example of this is Francis Costello's (character played by Jack Nicholson) obsession with having rats in his "family" in the film *The Departed*.

[2] The origin of this meaning might be found in the Bible, specifically in the Book of Genesis.

[3] This use of *ape* ignores the fact that humans are apes too.

FROM PEST TO PETS

It is worth noting that, as infamous as the rat is among us, in the Western culture, the feeling is not universal. In Eastern cultures this animal has a better name. This is the case with the Chinese culture, which places the rat in the first position of the zodiac, followed by the ox, tiger, rabbit, dragon, snake, horse, sheep (or goat), monkey, rooster, dog, and pig (or boar), with each animal (of course, assuming the dragon was accepted as such) representing one of the twelve Earthly Branches or, for practical purposes, one year in a twelve-year cycle. Interestingly, the rat leads the cycle in the Chinese calendar because of its intelligence. It was only thanks to its cunning that the rat could win the legendary race officiated by the Jade Emperor against such admirable opponents.

Supposedly, the twelve animals fought over the precedence of the animals in the cycle of years in the calendar, so the Chinese gods held a contest to determine the order. All the animals lined up on the bank of a river and were given the task of getting to the opposite shore. Their order in the calendar would be set by the order in which the animals managed to reach the other side. The cat wondered how he would get across if he was afraid of water. At the same time, the ox wondered how he would cross with his poor eyesight. The calculating rat suggested that he and the cat jump onto the ox's back and guide him across. The ox was steady and hard-working so that he did not notice a commotion on his back. In the meanwhile, the rat sneaked up behind the unsuspecting cat and shoved him into the water. Just as the ox came ashore, the rat jumped off and finished the race first. The lazy pig came to the far shore in twelfth place. And so the rat got the first year named after him, the ox got the second year, and the pig ended up as the last year in the cycle. The cat finished too late to win any place in the calendar, and vowed to be the enemy of the rat forevermore.[4]

---

[4] Retrieved on 01/25/2010 from Wikipedia (http://tinyurl.com/ygaxe97). Also see Young
(Footnote continued on next page)

In another legend, the cat asked the rat to wake him up for the race, but the rat reportedly "forgot" to do so. (No matter what, the cat always had good reasons to hold a grudge against the tricky rat.) In any case, it is interesting to note that, only by being "intelligent and cunning at the same time" (attributes of the rat in the Chinese zodiac) could an animal otherwise associated with "death, war, the occult, pestilence, and atrocities" in the Chinese tradition win the race. But the Chinese culture is not the only one that venerates rats:

> *In Indian tradition rats are recognized as the vehicle of Lord Ganesh and a rat's statue is always found in a temple of Ganesh. In the northwestern Indian city of Deshnoke, the rats at the Karni Mata Temple are held to be destined for reincarnation as Sadhus (Hindu holy men). The attending priests feed milk and grain to the rats, of which the pilgrims also partake. Eating food that has been touched by rats is considered a blessing from god.*[5]

There might be a good reason why the rat happens to have a better name in Eastern cultures (such as the Chinese and Indian cultures), than in our Western culture: Eastern cultures are ancestral cultures that evolved before certain historical events involving the rat took place. The reason why Westerners view the rat as a disgusting animal is mostly historical, and dates to the 1340s, when millions of Europeans lost their lives during the horrifying spread of the *Black Death*. This pandemic, also known as *Black Plague, Great Plague*, or *Great Pestilence*, presumably began in Central Asia and spread to Europe. It left in its wake an estimated 75 million deaths worldwide, including an estimated 20 to 30 million death toll in Europe alone. The prevailing theory on the Black Death relates it to an epidemic of *bubonic plague* (a name due to the buboes or swellings

---

(1998).

[5] Retrieved on 01/25/2010 from Wikipedia (http://tinyurl.com/2vaw9y3).

that it caused on a victim's neck, armpits, and/or groin). According to this theory, although the rat was not responsible for this deadly pandemic, its role was quite relevant. The Black Death was presumably caused by a kind of bacteria named *Yersinia pestis*, injected in the human bloodstream by the bite of the rat flea (*Xenopsylla cheopis*). Thus, the rat (more specifically, the oriental rat), was a carrier of the agent causing the disease (a *vector*, as they call this in biology), not the direct cause of the disease. But what could our European ancestors understand about the real causes of their worst nightmare? What they saw was a black rat (the rat introduced in Europe by trade was black, the *Rattus rattus*) which preceded the deadly symptoms (among them, black hemorrhagic splotches that gave the plague its name[6]). Had they known, in the 14th century, what really caused the disease, maybe the rat's reputation would be different. Or perhaps this knowledge would make no difference: after all, the rat would still be considered a very reliable signal, an omen even, of a horrible death. In any case, rats are now thought to be filthy animals in which parasites live at large.

In our overpopulated cities, rats still live among us, usually underground, sometimes taking over buildings, and farms[7]. For some, rats are just an annoyance, for others they are a serious risk[8]. With a *curriculum vitae* that looks more like a criminal record, it is not surprising that rats are still considered repulsive pests that threaten to infest our homes and carry all kinds of microbes and that, consequently, rat extermination or its polite synonym, *rat control*, is still a business in great demand by city dwellers.

But not everyone hates rats. There are a handful of people

---

[6] See Winn, Allen, Janda, Koneman, Schreckenberger, Procop, and Woods (2006) for a thorough description of the symptoms of the bubonic plague.

[7] Sullivan (2004).

[8] In February 2007, a baby lost part of her face after being bitten by rats while sleeping in her crib in Kansas City (http://tinyurl.com/5325fz).

who actually *love* them... and the number of rat lovers seems to be growing. Their passion for the rat (well, the *fancy rat*, as they call their pet) is so intense that they have even founded associations to promote "the breeding and exhibition of fancy rats and mice for show and pets"[9]. If you visit a website devoted to those who have rats as pets, you will notice that they speak about them with great anthropomorphic tenderness: expressions like "little guys", "little fellas", and "little ratties" are usually surrounded by descriptions of the personalities of these animals (their owners' interpretation of their pets' behavior in terms of human-like personalities), and the word *love* in multiple forms[10].

Now, the reader might be wondering *why would I want to have such a dirty and aggressive critter in my home?* The answer is very simple: because domesticated rats are neither dirty nor aggressive. Anyone who has had rats, either at home or in the laboratory, finds it surprising at first how much time rats devote to cleanliness. Rats groom very frequently[11], both themselves (*autogrooming*) and each other (*allogrooming*, typically seen in mothers with their pups). Observing their grooming behavior is always a pleasure: such painstaking licking of their fur, inspecting spots with impossible contortions, and washing their faces all the way behind their ears. (If only the human species devoted so much attention to personal hygiene as rats do!) Regarding their presumed aggressiveness, rats are no more aggressive than other domesticated animals. Sure, they can bite... but so can dogs and cats. As rodents, rats' teeth grow continuously and must be worn down by biting continuously

---

[9] See the website of the American Fancy Rat & Mouse Association at http://www.afrma.org, as well as its even fancier British sister at http://www.nfrs.org.

[10] There are dozens of websites of this sort, but I found this one to be especially heartfelt and quite complete: http://tinyurl.com/ybh9dbv.

[11] Almost one third of their waking life, according to some sources (http://tinyurl.com/yfd7x9c), although this, apparently, is not enough for some rat fans (http://tinyurl.com/ygpxw87).

(*gnawing*), usually on very hard objects, such as plastics or even metal. But this does not mean rats are blood-thirsty killers in a cheap horror movie. Rats do sometimes bite people, true, but they usually do so when feeling cornered and only as a last resort. When facing the fight or flight dilemma, they often go with the latter option – unless there is no other choice.

Coincidentally, as I write these lines (January 2008), the rats-as-pets fashion happens to be rapidly spreading in Western culture, mostly for two reasons. One has to do with the upcoming Year of the Rat in the Chinese calendar (February 7, 2008), which apparently makes it a good reason to buy a rat in Russia[12]. The other event had to do with a movie (nothing better than a movie when it comes to virally propagating a new fashion amongst our youngsters), the Pixar/Disney co-production *Ratatouille*[13]. Because this movie happens to tell of the adventures of a French rat in Paris, French and, especially, Parisian kids have gone crazy about rats. This usually translates into using any available tactic to get their parents to buy a rat for them[14]. Such is the power of a movie or, at least, a Disney movie (thankfully, this sudden interest in rats among our children was not inspired by the movie *Willard*[15]). Because these two fashions, as any other fashion, will be pretty ephemeral, we should not be surprised if the cities of Moscow and Paris soon have to deal with a big rat-problem on their streets. For an animal that weans at the age of 21 days, that reaches sexual maturity at 40-60 days of age, that has a gestation period of 21-22 days and a litter

---

[12] This news has received widespread attention in the media, especially on the Internet: http://tinyurl.com/yz7spxa, http://tinyurl.com/ywxo6u, http://tinyurl.com/ylg7km2, and http://tinyurl.com/yk4mpju.

[13] See http://www.imdb.com/title/tt0382932.

[14] This news has also received huge attention: http://tinyurl.com/ykdjcj5, http://tinyurl.com/26nj2d, http://tinyurl.com/mhlbof, http://tinyurl.com/ytr3r2, http://tinyurl.com/yh69kco, and http://tinyurl.com/yl35b3d.

[15] See http://www.imdb.com/title/tt0310357.

size of 6-14, with females reaching the reproductive senescence (meaning, that they cannot reproduce anymore) at the age of 15-24 months, and that has a life-span of 2-3.5 years[16] – in other words, for an animal that is specialized in multiplying and spreading (or infesting, depending on the viewpoint), this should be no problem.

THE ALBINO RAT FAMILY: WHITE AND TAME

The family of the rat is relatively large[17], with 56 known species in the rat genus (*Rattus*). The most common species in Western countries is the black rat (*Rattus rattus*) and the brown rat (*Rattus norvegicus*, sometimes spelled as *norwegicus*, and also known as the *Norway rat* or *Norwegian rat*). The black rat (also commonly referred to as the *home rat*, the *roof rat*, the *ship rat*, or the *Alexandrine rat*), which was previously mentioned in relation to its role the Black Death pandemic, originated in Asia and first spread to Europe in the 6th century to, then, colonize the rest of the world. The black rat specialized in warm areas, being replaced in cooler areas by the brown rat (also referred to as the *common rat*, and the *wharf rat*). The brown rat also originated in Asia and spread over Europe and North America in the 18th century. If you ever came across a wild rat in your lifetime, chances are this is the rat you saw, since it is the one that inhabits our cities[18].

The laboratory rat is a descendent of the *Rattus norvegicus*. In the early 1800s, the brown rat was caught and kept in captivity mostly for its use in rat-baiting, a popular sport of the British Victorian times[19]. Around the 1840s and 1860s, rats were bred and

---

[16] This data is borrowed from Quinn (2005) and Pass and Freeth (1993).

[17] See Barnett (2001) and visit Wikipedia at http://tinyurl.com/yzdvm4w.

[18] See Sullivan (2004) and visit Wikipedia at http://tinyurl.com/h34qr.

[19] See Boakes (1984), Pass and Freeth (1993), and http://tinyurl.com/yz6cceq.

sold as pets. The albino mutant then became popular. The albino rat, also known as Pink-Eyed White[20] (PEW) rat among those who have fancy rats, eventually made its way into the laboratory. In fact, the rat was the first mammalian ever domesticated for scientific research. Although rats were being already used in experiments in France around 1860, the albino rat became the standard experimental subject in the life sciences[21] when the Wistar Institute, located on the campus of the University of Pennsylvania, developed their outbred strain of the brown rat: the Wistar rat. Soon after the first commercial colony of Wistar rats was established at the Wistar Institute in 1906, this rat became part of the colonies in laboratories all over the world. Other popular strains (or *models,* as they are typically referred to[22]) were then developed[23]. The Sprague-Dawley (SD) strain was "born" at Harlan Sprague Dawley Inc. (Indianapolis, IN) from Wistar females and a "hybrid" male of unknown origin. Telling a Sprague-Dawley rat from a Wistar is not easy for the occasional observer, for they both are completely white and pink-eyed. However, adult rats of the Sprague-Dawley strain are typically smaller than adult Wistar rats. Sprague-Dawley rats are also more docile and calmer, which makes them easier to handle. Another popular strain in research is the Long-Evans, a strain that is believed to be the product of crossing Wistar females with a wild brown male rat, and was developed by Joseph Long and Herbert Evans between 1915 and 1920 at the University of California at

---

[20] The "pink" color (red is more appropriate) of their eyes, as their white fur, is due to albinism, specifically to the underlying retinal blood vessels, which are not covered by the pigment normally present in non-albino rats.

[21] For the use of the rat as a standard experimental subject in biomedical research, see Gill, Smith, Wissler, and Kunz (1989).

[22] The term *model* comes from *model organism* or *animal model.* The reason is simple: these animals are used as models of us, humans.

[23] A comprehensive list of the different rat strains available for research can be found at http://tinyurl.com/yfwujg8. Main providers of rat models in the United States are Charles River Laboratories, Inc. (http://www.criver.com) and Harlan Sprague Dawley, Inc. (http://www.harlan.com).

Berkeley[24]. This rat is easier to spot due to its black and white colored fur: with a black head and upper back (it has black eyes too), and a white abdominal region, this rat looks like a Wistar with a black hood (hence, its alternative name *black hooded*). Its black head and upper back makes the Long-Evans the perfect candidate for studies in which its movements on an open space are recorded on video. In conditions in which its "cousins" would be hard to spot, such as in a circular swimming pool filled with whitened water (as it is typical in the Morris water-maze), the Long-Evans rat is conspicuous, revealing its position in sharp black-and-white.

BRAIN IN A NUTSHELL

An adult human brain weighs, on average, 1300-1400 g (around 3 pounds). Assuming an average total body weight of 68 kg (around 150 pounds) for a human adult, this means that our brain is responsible for about 2% of our total body weight. An adult rat weighs, on average, 400 g and its brain weighs, on average, 2 g. This means that the rat's brain accounts for about 0.5% of its body weight[25]. They are tiny animals with really tiny brains indeed. So, what can we expect from a brain of the size of a nut? With an estimated average of 21 million neurons in its cerebral cortex[26], there must be some computational power a rat can afford. This book (especially Chapters 3-5) will be devoted to discuss a few amazing feats of such a tiny biological microprocessor.

---

[24] Suckow, Weisbroth, and Franklin (2006).

[25] Data from http://tinyurl.com/63won8.

[26] Korbo, Pakkenberg, Ladefoged, Gundersen, Arlien-Søborg, and Pakkenberg (1990).

CHAPTER 2: THE LABORATORY RAT

In this chapter I discuss the historical events that resulted in the ubiquity of the rat in the animal psychology laboratory, from *behaviorism* to *cognitive psychology*. Digging through the history of psychology will give us a better understanding of the importance of recent studies that show complex cognitive processes in the rat. It is my intention to keep this discussion brief and simple, so rather than really digging in, we will just scratch the surface in search for the main events, ideas, and people relevant to the story at hand: how the rat became the standard subject in the psychology laboratory.

RATS IN THE SPOTLIGHT

"They are small, cheap, easily fed and cared for"[1]. With these words, Colin C. Stewart, a biologist at Clark University convinced Linus Ward Kline, a psychology instructor, of using rats in his laboratory of comparative psychology. It was then 1897, and this still seems to be the best way to put it. The rat became the champion of the psychology laboratory because of its reduced size (hence, one can house many animals in a small laboratory... and psychology laboratories are rarely large), low price (another good reason, especially for modest laboratories), and easy maintenance (also reducing costs in food and animal care staff). But, still, the question applies: why the rat? There are certainly hundreds, if not thousands of other animals that could have been chosen as research models in the psychology laboratory based on the criteria of size, price, and maintenance. Here is another reason: the rat is a mammal, a warm-blooded animal and, thus, evolutionarily close

---

[1] See Stewart (1898), p. 41. This text is also quoted on p. 143 of Boakes (1984) and on p. 28 of Lemov (2005), both of which also served as the main source for this section.

enough to us, humans, that researchers could draw conclusions about human behavior. At the same time, the rat was viewed as a "lower" animal that did not inspire much sympathy, so a researcher could perform multiple experimental treatments, most of which would be seen as inhumane in "higher" animals, such as primates.

The rat arrived in American laboratories with Swiss psychiatrist Adolf Meyer. In 1892, Meyer moved to the United States to contact Henry Herbert Donaldson, a professor of neurology and a pioneer in experimental psychology at the University of Chicago. Soon after arriving in Chicago, Meyer imported his first laboratory rats. Meyer convinced Donaldson of the many advantages of using rats to study the nervous system. By the time Meyer left the University of Chicago for his new job at Clark University in 1895, Donaldson had a rat colony with animals yielded by Meyer[2]. At Clark too, Meyer soon convinced other researchers of the advantages of using rats – among them, Stewart, the biologist who, in turn, convinced Linus Kline with the persuasive arguments that opened this section. Kline used rats in comparative psychology studies and supervised a graduate student, Willard Stanton Small, whose work was focused on associative processes in the rat. Although Kline went to Clark with the only purpose of studying animals, his plans were frustrated by Stanley Hall, a psychologist with great power (at that time, Hall was the first president of, not only Clark University, but also the American Psychological Association, or APA, which was founded in 1892 at Clark). In the end, Small happened to be remembered as the first person using rats in a psychology experiment.

Small is also known for building the first maze to study learning in rats (he used the maze at the Hampton Court Palace as a

---

[2] Donaldson became the first American scientist to work with rats (in physiology) and later, in 1906, established a colony of rats in the Wistar Institute, from which the Wistar strain descended.

model). In his studies[3], rats were constantly exposed to the maze (they actually lived in it) and their knowledge of the labyrinthine corridors was assessed from their ability to reach, while hungry, the center of the maze, where the experimenter had placed food. In this condition, the time to reach the food as well as the number of errors in the turns were registered and analyzed, with these indexes of behavior being interpreted as indicative of learning. However, these initial studies were mostly observational and, thus, they lacked the manipulation of independent variables and control of potentially spurious variables (essential features of the experimental method). Also, in his 1901 publication, Small made multiple inferences on the presumed subjective experiences of the animals. For example, he claimed that "one could not fail to see that the rat was trying to select his path – there seemed to be some kind of an image in his mind that he was trying to follow" (p. 212); "This acceleration was accompanied by a flick of the tail and a general abandon that said, 'I've struck the right trail.'" (p. 213); and that the rat "apparently knew when he was on the right and when on the wrong road." (p. 213).

In spite of the relevance of Small's pioneer work, due to APA president Stanley Hall's interests in other areas of psychology, such as developmental psychology (*aka* child psychology) and abnormal psychology, psychological experiments with animals at Clark University were short-lived (they ended soon after 1900). This brings us back to the University of Chicago, were Donaldson still kept rats in his laboratory; the only psychology laboratory in America holding rats at the time. As in many things in life, what happened next was the result of a fortuitous event, but with profound consequences nevertheless: Donaldson hired a young, ambitious student in great need of money. This student was already working as an assistant janitor, cleaning the apparatuses in the

---

[3] Small (1901).

laboratory of one of his mentors (James Angell), while also delivering newspapers and waiting tables. The importance of the consequences of Donaldson's hire are easier to understand once it is mentioned that the job consisted of caring for his white rats, and that this ambitious student was John B. Watson.

WATSON'S BEHAVIORISM AND THE CRAZE FOR THE WHITE RAT

Many historical accounts portray John Broadus Watson as a very intense man, with a very intense life[4]. Everywhere his name appears, events of great interest for the casual reader follow. He is the man who conducted the famous (or infamous, depending on the reader's viewpoint) "Little Albert" experiment[5] with Rosalie Rayner, a shocking demonstration of fear conditioning in a 9-month-old baby (Albert) which (to the joy of some, and the horror of others) also happened to be videotaped. He is also the man who lost his faculty position at Johns Hopkins University, because of an affair with his graduate assistant, Rosalie Rayner, which happened to get too much public attention. He is also famous for his radical ideas on what psychology should be, namely, a science of behavior (*behaviorism*), in which there is no room for introspection and in which all animal behavior, human and nonhuman, can be explained in terms of the relations between the stimuli in the environment and the responses they elicit in the organism. His behaviorist philosophy was made clear in his 1913 publication, commonly known as the *behaviorist manifesto*, in which the opening paragraph became an instant classic for its being straightforward, simple, and (for the prevailing paradigm of the time) mind-boggling:

---

[4] As in the preceding section, the sources for this section are the books by Boakes (1984) and Lemov (2005), which I strongly recommend.

[5] Watson and Rayner (1920).

Psychology as the behaviorist views it is a purely objective experimental branch of natural science. Its theoretical goal is the prediction and control of behavior. Introspection forms no essential part of its methods, nor is the scientific value of its data dependent upon the readiness with which they lend themselves to interpretation in terms of consciousness. The behaviorist, in his efforts to get a unitary scheme of animal response, recognizes no dividing line between man and brute. The behavior of man, with all of its refinement and complexity, forms only a part of the behaviorist's total scheme of investigation.[6]

Because his manifesto proclaimed "a unitary scheme of animal response" with "no dividing line between man and brute", the use of animals in the psychology laboratory made perfect sense to Watson. When Watson found himself, as a graduate student, caring for Donaldson's rat colony at the University of Chicago, he already had some clear ideas in mind. He knew, for example, that philosophy did not make much sense to him, even when the primary reason why he went to the University of Chicago was to take philosophy classes with John Dewey. His interest in philosophy had already been replaced with an interest in neurophysiology, especially after he worked with the biologist and physiologist Jacques Loeb. Of great impact on Watson was Loeb's research on animal tropisms, or the growth or turning movement of an organism in response to an environmental stimulus, such as light, humidity, or gravity. Thus, when he started working with rats in psychology, he already had a well-defined approach: to study the behavior of the rat in terms of responses to stimuli, with no reference to mental states in the animal; a pure stimulus-response (or S-R) account.

This is not to claim that Watson "invented" the S-R account of behavior. This notion dates from the dualist view of René

---

[6] Watson (1913).

Descartes, who proposed that involuntary behaviors are automatic reactions to external stimuli, mediated by what he called *reflex*. Later on, Russian physiologist Ivan M. Sechenov extended the concept of reflex to mental processes and, thereby, proposed a physiological account of psychology (in which the concept of *inhibition* played a major role). But it was Russian physiologist Ivan Petrovich Pavlov, who brought the S-R account of behavior to psychology, due to his serendipitous discovery of the *conditional reflexes*, most commonly known as *conditioned reflexes*[7], during his research on the processes of digestion in dogs, which ultimately awarded him the Nobel Prize in Physiology[8] in 1904.

The story of how Pavlov discovered the conditioned reflexes can be found in almost any psychology textbook. Here is a short version of this story: in his studies on the digestion of dogs, Pavlov surgically implanted artificial tubes (fistulas or *fistulae*) in live dogs to collect their digestive juices. His technicians soon realized that the dogs secreted stomach juices, not only in response to the ingestion of food (meat powder), but also in response to the sight of food, or even to the person who usually fed them. They called these secretions *psychic secretions* because of their being produced by food-related stimuli. For years, although these psychic secretions remained unstudied, they were sold to the general public as a remedy for various stomach ailments, a business that provided supplementary income to the laboratory[9]. It was not until S. G. Vul'fson and A. T. Snarskii decided to systematically study the psychic reflexes in the salivary glands in Pavlov's laboratory, that research on the conditioned reflexes finally became a priority. Both Vul'fson and Snarskii used a surgical procedure consisting of implanting a fistula in specific salivary glands, and then studied the

---

[7] Due to a mistranslation in the first English edition (see Domjan, 2009, p. 71).

[8] Visit http://tinyurl.com/yfhw9ql.

[9] Domjan (2009), p. 69.

salivation produced by the placement of several substances (food, flavored water) in the dog's mouth, as well as the salivation produced by the mere sight of these substances after repeated exposure to the food. Pavlov saw the implications of these studies, but wanted to go even further. He wanted to study the conditioned response elicited by stimuli that were independent of the food (in the experiments of Vul'fson and Snarskii, conditioned responses were produced by features of the food, such as their visual characteristics). Thus, Pavlov created a paradigm in which the salivary conditioned response could be elicited by arbitrary stimuli unrelated to the food stimulus, such as a sound[10]. Although the sound was initially neutral, after several pairings with the food presentation, it elicited a response that resembled the response produced by the ingestion of food itself. That is, the dogs learned to salivate to the sound that signaled the food presentation. At this time, the sound is referred to as a *conditioned stimulus* (CS), due to its producing a response which is conditional upon its pairings with the food stimulus[11]. This response is referred to as the *conditioned response* (CR). Because the food stimulus elicited a response with no need of prior training, it is referred to as an *unconditioned stimulus* (US), which elicits an *unconditioned response* (UR).

The importance of Pavlov's paradigm (known as *classical* or *Pavlovian conditioning*) was soon realized by Watson, who applied it to Little Albert in the first fear conditioning experiment ever conducted using a human subject[12]. In this experiment, 9-month-old Albert was repeatedly exposed to a white laboratory rat while a steel bar was hit with a hammer behind his head (out of Albert's view).

---

[10] Despite the typical account of Pavlov's paradigm as involving the use of a ringing bell (Tully, 2003), it seems that Pavlov rarely used one (Black, 2003).

[11] The terms *CS* and *CR* make more sense if we keep in mind that they originally meant *conditional stimulus* and *conditional response*, respectively (Domjan, 2009, p. 71).

[12] Watson and Rayner (1920).

The pairing of the rat (CS) with the loud noise (US), which Albert was afraid of (UR), resulted in the rat also eliciting a fear response (CR). This fear response then generalized to other things that resembled the white rat (white furry things, such as a rabbit or cotton). Watson was fully convinced that our personalities are no more than a collection of S-R associations we have acquired since our early years and, thus, that Pavlovian conditioning could be used to engineer any kind of human being. This point is made clear in his famous "twelve infants" quote:

> *Give me a dozen healthy infants, well-formed, and my own specified world to bring them up in and I'll guarantee to take any one at random and train him to become any type of specialist I might select – doctor, lawyer, artist, merchant-chief and, yes, even beggar-man and thief, regardless of his talents, penchants, tendencies, abilities, vocations, and race of his ancestors.*[13]

Watson's philosophy of psychology, behaviorism, was very straightforward. As someone who was frustrated with the ill-defined approach to psychology of his time, which mainly relied on introspection as a research method[14], Watson found in Pavlov's S-R framework the basis for his empirically-oriented psychology[15]. Importantly, he proposed that this new psychology could provide us with the tools to, not only understand behavior, but to also change it. The possibility of having a tool for systematically changing behavior might be one of the reasons why Watson's behaviorism became so popular. Psychologists were already in the enterprise of understanding the human mind, but Watson's fresh

---

[13] Watson (1924/1997), p. 82.

[14] Such was the approach of Wilhelm Wundt, founder of the first laboratory of experimental psychology at the University of Leipzig, Germany, in 1879.

[15] The obsession of behaviorism with relying on observable events (stimuli and responses) while rejecting introspection was neatly captured in an old joke: "One behaviorist to another after lovemaking: 'Darling, that was wonderful for you. How was it for me?'"

new approach to psychology came with the promise of behavioral change, something that more than a few soon linked to another, darker possibility: behavioral control[16].

Behaviorist psychology was concerned with simple laws governing human behavior, namely those by which the pairings of certain stimuli result in the formation of S-R associations. Once the S-R association had been formed, one only had to present the stimulus to elicit the desired response. Whatever happened in between the stimulus (S) and the response (R) was not a relevant object of study, it actually did not matter. Thus, in this new psychology, using "lower" animals in the psychology laboratory did not need much justification. Because the laws of associative learning were presumed to explain both human and nonhuman behavior, one could perfectly study the behavior of relatively simple animals in the laboratory to, then, draw conclusions about human behavior. Contrary to the experimental use of humans, using animals had many advantages. First, the influence of instinctive responses was less likely to confound the results, given that one could use animals from the same "family" (strain). Second, all animals had a similar history prior to the experiment and, hence, this factor was also less likely to spoil the results. Third, during the experiment, animals could be placed for extended periods of time in well-controlled environments. Fourth, one could perform treatments on animals that were impossible or unethical on humans (for example, depriving them of food and/or water, giving them electric shocks or mild doses of a poison). And, fifth, the results from animal experiments were easier to interpret than those involving humans.

In sum, Watson's behaviorism popularized the use of animals in the psychology laboratory. During the first decades of the 20th century, more and more psychologists turned their attention to

---

[16] Lemov's (2005) book will satisfy those who want to learn more about this latter aspect.

"lower" animals, in search of clues to understand human behavior. Among the many animals one could find in the psychology laboratory of the time (for example, dogs, cats, chicken, goats, monkeys, pigeons...), the rat soon became the most popular choice. A few decades later, the rat was running mazes in psychology laboratories at universities all around the world and, especially, the United States. Precisely in this country, another great scientist would soon play a big role in this story: Burrhus Frederic Skinner, the man whose research gave behaviorism the ultimate push, and who standardized the use of the rat in psychology... by *putting it in a box*.

RATS IN BOXES: SKINNER'S OPERANT CONDITIONING

Contrary to Watson, B. F. Skinner was not centrally interested in Pavlovian or classical conditioning, which he referred to as *respondent* conditioning. Instead, Skinner was interested in the kind of behavior he referred to as *operant behavior* and, more specifically, in the processes by which these responses are acquired and modified: *operant conditioning*. A comprehensive discussion of Skinner's ideas, which he delivered in more than 200 publications[17], would require a book on its own (and, in fact, many books about Skinner's life and work have been written). Here I briefly discuss a selection of some of his ideas, a selection that will also serve the purpose of introducing some of the concepts and experimental methods currently in use in psychology and, thus, necessary to understand the research reviewed in the next chapters[18].

---

[17] A complete list of his publications can be found at http://tinyurl.com/29bjqfa.

[18] The reader interested in learning more about Skinner's work will find plenty of information in textbooks of learning and behavior (for example, Bouton, 2007; Domjan, 2009) and of history of psychology (for example, Leahey, 2004). Also, Skinner himself

(Footnote continued on next page)

Let us start with the distinction between Pavlovian conditioning (*aka* classical or respondent conditioning) and operant conditioning. On one hand, classically conditioned responses (respondents) are typically automatic, uncontrollable responses that are triggered by specific stimuli. Examples of respondents include salivation, eye blinking, knee-jerk, or emotional responses such as fear or sexual arousal. That is, respondents are responses that are *elicited* by the conditioned stimulus. On the other hand, operant responses are "voluntary" behaviors[19] that allow us to produce an impact on our environment, be it physical or social. That is, operant behaviors are responses that are *emitted* by the organism in its interaction with the environment. Examples of operant responses include most of our daily activities: reading a book, driving a car, picking up the phone, talking to someone, buying groceries, watching TV, going to work, or even procrastinating big time.

The environmental impact of operant behaviors is central to these responses. In fact, Skinner defined operant behaviors based on the effect that they have on the environment. For example, the simple operant behavior *turning the lights on* is not described in terms of the actions being performed (one could flip the switch with a finger or with one's nose), but in terms of what happens when the behavior is performed: the switch is closed, electricity flows from one contact to the other, and the bulbs light up.

Skinner's extensive work on operant conditioning was that of a hard-working genius, but it was not totally original. In fact, many of his ideas were inspired on Edward Lee Thorndike's original work on instrumental learning[20]. More specifically, Skinner's work was

provided a brief survey of his work in a paper available at http://tinyurl.com/yzcadq9.

[19] Skinner denied the existence of volition or free-will. In his view, no behavior was voluntary, but determined by its consequences and controlled by its antecedents.

[20] Thorndike used the term *instrumental learning* because these behaviors were instrumental in producing a desired outcome, whereas Skinner chose the term *operant conditioning* because this behavior allows the organism to operate upon its environment. Nevertheless, these

(Footnote continued on next page)

built upon Thorndike's famous *Law of Effect*:

> *The Law of Effect is that: Of several responses made to the same situation, those which are accompanied or closely followed by satisfaction to the animal will, other things being equal, be more firmly connected with the situation, so that, when it recurs, they will be more likely to recur; those which are accompanied or closely followed by discomfort to the animal will, other things being equal, have their connections with that situation weakened, so that, when it recurs, they will be less likely to occur. The greater the satisfaction or discomfort, the greater the strengthening or weakening of the bond.* [21]

Skinner agreed with Thorndike's Law of Effect but, as a man who always avoided any references to internal, subjective states in the animal, framed it in purely observable terms. In his revised version of the Law of Effect, Skinner introduced the concepts of *reinforcement* and *punishment*. By reinforcement, Skinner referred to the strengthening of a behavior due to the consequences it produces. A behavior is said to be reinforced or strengthened when the probability or frequency of its occurrence increases, when it is performed more intensely, and/or when it happens more readily (the delay or latency in its performance becomes shorter). For example, a student giving a personal opinion in class might receive the attention and praise of the professor in return and, thus, be more likely to provide her opinions again during the class time. In this case, sharing personal opinions is an operant response that has been reinforced, with the professor's attention and praise being *appetitive stimuli*, typically referred to as the *reinforcers* of this behavior.

Another central concept in Skinner's work is *punishment*, which is defined as the weakening of a behavior due to the

---

two terms refer to the same process, and are now used interchangeably.

[21] Thorndike (1911), p. 244. Incidentally, Skinner did not cite Thorndike's work in his *The behavior of organisms* (Skinner, 1938), something for which he then profusely apologized in a letter (see Pear, 2007, p. 110).

consequences it produces. Specifically, when the response produces a stimulus that causes the response to be suppressed in the future (that is, less likely to happen, less intense, longer delay/latency, etc.), punishment is said to happen. The stimulus causing the response suppression is referred to as an *aversive stimulus* or *punisher*. To continue with the previous example, the student's behavior consisting of giving her personal opinion in class could also be perceived by the professor as an annoying interruption of the lecture. In this case, the verbal and nonverbal stimuli in the professor's reaction would ideally reduce the likelihood that the student will share her opinions during class time in the future, in which case the professor's reaction is said to have effectively punished the student's behavior.

In the previous discussion of reinforcement and punishment, the consequences of the operant behavior consisted of the presentation of a stimulus (the reinforcer and the punisher, respectively). In these two cases, a *positive contingency* or relationship was established between the occurrence of the response and the occurrence of the stimulus: if, and only if, the response was emitted, the stimulus was presented. However, a *negative contingency* can also be established. In this case, when the response is emitted, a stimulus that is otherwise present or scheduled to occur is removed from the environment. Interestingly, the removal of a stimulus can also serve to reinforce a response. Specifically, this happens when a response eliminates from the environment an aversive stimulus (or punisher). This is called *negative reinforcement*. Take again the example of the student sharing personal opinions in class. Let us imagine that the class is painfully tedious from the student's perspective (certainly not a stretch of the imagination to many) and that, every time the student intervenes to tell her personal opinion, the professor stops his lecture for a few minutes. The interruption of the lecture (an aversive stimulus in this case) functions as a negative reinforcer for the student's behavior of sharing an opinion. This specific instance of negative reinforcement is also referred to as *escape*, because the response interrupts an ongoing aversive stimulus (it removes the stimulus). In the other instance of negative reinforcement, the response prevents the occurrence of the aversive stimulus. In this case we speak of *avoidance*. This would be the case if the student started sharing opinions from the first minute, even before the professor had a chance to start his lecture.

Finally, a negative contingency can also be established between the response and a reinforcer. In this case, referred to as *negative punishment* or *omission training*, the response removes from the environment an appetitive stimulus and it is thereby weakened. Continuing with the previous example, let us assume that the professor's lecture can only be described as thrilling and fun (remember, this is a fictitious scenario, so anything is possible). In that case, each time the student shares an opinion and causes the professor to interrupt the lecture, moments of indescribably fulfilling intellectual insights are forever lost. As a consequence, the behavior of the student will decrease in the future.

In sum, there are four main types of operant conditioning procedures, resulting from the combination of the contingency or relationship that is established between the operant response and its outcome (positive or negative) and the motivational nature of the outcome (appetitive or aversive). These four procedures are summarized in the following table.

	Appetitive outcome	Aversive outcome
Positive contingency	Positive reinforcement (or simply *reinforcement*)	Positive punishment (or simply *punishment*)
Negative contingency	Negative punishment or omission training	Negative reinforcement (escape and avoidance)

Skinner also differed from Thorndike at a theoretical level. According to Thorndike, instrumental learning consists of the formation of a connection (a *bond*, as he called it) between the stimuli present in the environment and the instrumental response, with the consequence of the response just *stamping in* the S-R link. That is, Thorndike proposed an S-R account of instrumental learning, similar to Pavlov's account of classical conditioning. By contrast, Skinner's operant conditioning did not rely on the formation of S-R associations. As was previously stated, in Skinner's view operant responses were emitted by the organism, instead of automatically elicited by the stimuli present in the environment, as in the case of respondent conditioning. In Skinner's framework, the functional relationship between the response and its consequences was what determined the probability of the occurrence of the response, with the stimuli in the environment serving to signal when the consequence will occur, assuming that the response is emitted. Consider the following example: answering a phone (the operant response) usually results in somebody's voice on the speaker (the consequence), but only when it was previously ringing (the stimulus). The phone's ring, however, does not trigger an automatic response of picking up the phone in the same way the sight of food makes us salivate when we are hungry. Instead, the ring indicates to us that a certain reinforcer is available for performing a certain behavior. Accordingly, the stimulus preceding the response (the ring in this example) was referred to by Skinner as *discriminative stimulus*, because it helps us to discriminate the occasions on which the response will yield the consequence.

Skinner was also unhappy with Thorndike's experimental method. Thorndike's experiments used his ingenious *puzzle boxes*, in which a hungry animal (usually cats, but also dogs or chickens) was placed, with food very close to it, only outside the box. In order to get out of the box and enjoy the food, a specific response (pull a ring, press down a lever, etc.) had to be performed to release the latch locking the door. In his experimental setting, Thorndike could register the latency, or time the animal took to get out of the box, with changes in this latency being indicative of learning. In a typical experiment, the animal would progressively need less time (that is, a shorter latency) to complete the response needed to open the puzzle box. Basically, initial responses would be produced by mere *trial-and-error*, but eventually a response would produce the desired consequence and, as described in the Law of Effect, this response would be more likely to be performed again in the future. But Thorndike's experimental setting was far from perfect: on each trial, after the animal makes its way out to get to the food, the experimenter has to place the animal back into the apparatus. That is, it is a *discrete-trial* procedure, meaning that only one instrumental response can be produced on each experimental trial. In this sense, Thorndike's puzzle box did not show significant advantage over the maze. Skinner wanted to study operant behavior in a more naturalistic setting, in a situation in which the animal could freely produce an unlimited number of responses on each trial. In other words, he wanted a *free-operant* procedure for the study of behavior, and he achieved this procedure by devising his most famous apparatus: the Skinner box[22].

Skinner specifically designed his operant chamber for the study of operant behavior in the rat and the pigeon. In this chamber, isolated from external stimuli (the Skinner box is usually embedded in a sound-attenuating cubicle), the animal can perform specific operant responses, such as pressing down a lever (for rats) or pecking a key on a wall (for pigeons), which can result in the delivery of a reinforcer, such as food pellets (for rats) or grain (for pigeons), or water. Aversive stimuli can also be presented, usually consisting of an electric shock delivered through the floor grid[23].

---

[22] The term *Skinner box* was first used by Clark L. Hull (see Pear, 2007, p. 109). Skinner, however, was not fond of it and preferred the terms *experimental space, experimental apparatus, experimental chamber,* and *operant chamber* (Nye, 1992).

[23] The electric shocks employed in operant conditioning studies are weak (around 0.5 mA) and short (around 0.5 seconds). This is enough to produce discomfort without causing tissue damage.

Speakers and lights mounted on the walls and ceiling of the chamber allow the presentation of audiovisual stimuli that can serve as discriminative stimuli. In a typical operant conditioning experiment in the Skinner box, a rat would press down the bar in order to obtain a small food pellet after a tone had signaled the availability of food[24] (positive reinforcement) or, alternatively, the rat could press the bar in order to prevent the occurrence of the footshock, which is signaled by a light (negative reinforcement). The presentation of the different stimuli, as well as their duration and intensity, is completely controlled by the experimenter, who can also automatically record the animal's behavior. The experimental chamber, thus, means control and precision. It also means convenience and productivity: with the technology available today, one can connect up to sixteen Skinner boxes to a single personal computer and, thus, simultaneously run the experimental sessions with several animals. Once the experimenter has programmed the procedural details regarding the contingencies of reinforcement in the software controlling the experimental chambers, his presence in the experimental room is no longer necessary.

Although Skinner originally chose the rat as the experimental subject based on reasons of "convenience and control"[25], soon after he built his first operant chambers for the study of behavior in the rat, he abandoned the rat to focus on another species (the pigeon) as a better candidate for his research interests due to their "behav[ing] more rapidly than rats, allowing more rapid discoveries

---

[24] From the point of view of the rat, things might be different, as the joke goes: "A rat to another rat: 'I've trained my experimenter so that, every time I press this lever, he gives me a snack.'"

[25] Skinner explained his rationale for choosing the rat as follows:

> *In the broadest sense a science of behavior should be concerned with all kinds of organisms, but it is reasonable to limit oneself, at least in the beginning, to a single representative example. Through a certain anthropocentricity of interests we are likely to choose an organism as similar to man as is consistent with experimental convenience and control. The organism used here is the white rat.* (Skinner, 1938, p. 47; also cited, in part, by Lemov, 2005, pp. 36-37.)

of the effect of new contingencies"[26]. Those who closely followed Skinner's steps also chose the pigeon for their studies, but many researchers continued using the Skinner box with the white rat. The rat-box pair is still today ubiquitous in the animal psychology laboratory, especially in research conducted outside the Skinnerian tradition, generally known as *experimental analysis of behavior* or, simply, *behavior analysis*.

Skinner was a man of many talents. He was an excellent researcher, a creative genius when it came to inventing machines to make his work or daily life easier[27], and an effective writer with a great talent to communicate ideas in a simple, yet convincing manner. Always a scientist, he eventually became an influential philosopher. His philosophy was a behaviorism so radical that it made Watson's behaviorism look coy. Skinner was convinced that operant conditioning and, especially, reinforcement was not appropriately applied in our society, which relied excessively in punitive measures (for example, law enforcement). Skinner made important efforts in trying to communicate his ideas to the general public[28]; and to convince us that our society would have much to gain if it grew out of the ideal of free-will (which was just an illusion in his view) and embraced his proposal of a technology of behavior based on the techniques of operant conditioning[29].

---

[26] As described by Skinner's elder daughter, Julie Vargas, in her brief account of her father's biography (http://tinyurl.com/yzdw46f)

[27] In addition to the operant chamber, he also invented the cumulative record, a graphical record of the animal's behavior over time that could be connected to the operant chamber; and the *baby-tender* or *Aircrib*, an enclosed space, with controlled temperature and soundproof, where a baby could be comfortably left for a few hours (see Nye, 1992, pp. 7-8).

[28] A good example of this is his novel *Walden Two* (Skinner, 1948b).

[29] His controversial book *Beyond freedom and dignity* (Skinner, 1971) is devoted to this issue.

TOLMAN, AND THE FIRST COGNITIVE RAT

At the time Skinner's operant conditioning and radical behaviorism started to take off at Harvard, experiments were still being conducted with rats navigating mazes in the laboratories of many universities, including Edward Chace Tolman's laboratory at the University of California, Berkeley. In spite of his use of a more traditional experimental preparation, Tolman was "incubating" a theoretical approach that was everything but traditional. In fact, although technically speaking Tolman was a behaviorist (just not a typical behaviorist), Tolman' original viewpoint is now considered by many to be the precursor of what today is known as *cognitive psychology*[30].

Contrary to the radical behaviorism that Skinner was starting to develop at the time, and which declined to consider the role of any unobservable psychological process in behavior, Tolman[31] defended the use and study of unobservable events in psychology, provided that they were very well defined and carefully linked to external, observable events. He called these events *intervening variables*, because they presumably intervene between the environment and the behavior. The strength of his theoretical approach, known as *operational behaviorism*, was to allow unobservable events to play a role in behavior, but without losing the scrupulous scientific approach of behaviorism. In order to do so, any intervening variable had to be very carefully related to its antecedents (input) and its consequences (output). That is, the manipulation of the antecedents should have specific effects on the intervening variable, and the intervening variable should have, in

---

[30] See Knapp and Robertson (1986), p. 112. This opinion was even shared by Skinner, who commented regarding Tolman's approach in relation to his own: "That may have been the point at which the experimental analysis of behavior parted company from what would become cognitive psychology." (Richelle, 1993, p. 107).

[31] Tolman (1938).

turn, specific effects on the observable behavior.

Let us consider an example of a motivational intervening variable, *thirst*. As an unobservable event, speaking of thirst as a determinant of behavior could not meet the strict empirical standards of behaviorism[32]. Rather, the behaviorist preferred to speak of antecedent stimuli such as *water deprivation*, which could be directly manipulated and quantified (hours of water deprivation), and observable responses such as *water consumption*. That is, the behaviorist would stick to the S-R account of behavior. By contrast, in Tolman's operational behaviorism, the intervening variable *thirst* could be systematically related to the antecedents and the responses. In this case, it could be stated that increasing the number of hours of water deprivation would increase thirst which, in turn, would result in an increased amount of consumed water. This might be common sense for most of us now, but the reductionist approach of behaviorism would still see a problem here: if one can establish a functional relationship between two observable variables (number of hours of water deprivation and amount of water consumption), adding a third variable (thirst) seems an unnecessary complication, even more so when this variable cannot be directly observed. But, Tolman would claim, the addition of an intervening variable *does* make a difference. To begin with, it can tremendously simplify explanations. In the previous example, only one antecedent (water deprivation) and one consequence (water consumption) were discussed. But, what would happen if many variables were identified as antecedents and consequents? The picture would get messy. Consider the following figure[33].

---

[32] This is not to say that behaviorists denied the *existence* of these variables, they just claimed they were not necessary to study and explain behavior. Unobservable psychological processes (cognition, emotion, motivation) were referred to by Skinner as *third variables*, meaning that they play no causal role in the production of behavior (Richelle, 1993, p. 107).

[33] After Bouton (2007), p. 20, who, in turn, borrowed it from Miller (1959).

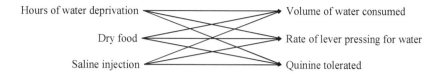

With three antecedent events (hours of water deprivation, intake of dry food, and a saline injection) being functionally related to three behavioral consequences (volume of water consumed, rate of lever pressing for water, and quinine tolerance), one could establish a total of nine links. This is what the "simple" approach of behaviorism would propose. Now, let us see what would happen if the intervening variable *thirst* was introduced between these antecedents and consequences.

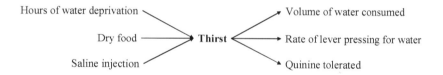

As can be seen in this figure[34], by assuming that a motivational variable, thirst, intervenes between the manipulations on the antecedents and the observed behavior, a clearer picture emerges, with six links, instead of nine. But, even more important than providing a simpler explanation of behavior, Tolman's intervening variables reinstated the importance of the organism (O), previously neglected in behaviorist psychology, which now was part of the S-R framework. He provided a new S-O-R theory of behavior.

---

[34] Ibid.

Tolman's work is of great relevance in the present discussion, not only because of his proposal of intervening variables in psychology, but also because his research made special emphasis on *cognitive* intervening variables. Other important researchers would later accept the usefulness of Tolman's operational behaviorism and propose internal mechanisms mediating in the S-R relationship[35]. For example, Clark L. Hull proposed the *drive*, meaning a motivation caused by a biological need, such as hunger or thirst, as a determinant of behavior. But, as a man whose ideas were ahead of his time, Tolman was a pioneer in proposing the determinant role of mental processes in the production of behavior. In fact, perhaps the most important intervening variable he ever proposed was the *cognitive map*. As Tolman stated in his article *Cognitive maps in rats and men* (a title that leaves no room for doubt about his theoretical view), the left or right turns of the rat in the maze were not viewed as simple responses to specific stimuli, but based on the animal's knowledge about the maze.

> *The stimuli, which are allowed in, are not connected by just simple one-to-one switches to the outgoing responses. Rather, the incoming impulses are usually worked over and elaborated in the central control room into a tentative, cognitive-like map of the environment. And it is this tentative map, indicating routes and paths and environmental relationships, which finally determines what responses, if any, the animal will finally release.*[36]

It is interesting to note that other important ideas in Tolman's work, which were at odds with contemporary mainstream views at the time, are ideas that most psychologists accept and share today. For example, he proposed that behavior is *goal-oriented*, that is

---

[35] Or, as brightly put by (Lemov, 2005), "the inarticulate "–" between "stimulus" and "response", p. 80.

[36] Tolman (1948), p. 192.

performed with a purpose[37], something that behaviorism strongly denied. Tolman also preferred to study meaningful, complex behavior (or *molar* behavior, such as searching for food), as opposed to the simple, almost irreducible behaviors (or *molecular* behavior, such as flexing a specific set of muscles to turn to the right) that were studied by behaviorists. And, finally, Tolman was the first one to introduce the *learning-performance* distinction, of great importance in current research in psychology of learning and behavior.

Let us consider this last point with more detail. In one of his most famous experiments[38], rats receiving a reward (food) for finding a goal location in a complex maze (condition R) performed better (they made fewer errors on average) over trials than rats that were never rewarded (condition NR). But this was not news. After all, such differences were consistent with the predictions of behaviorism, according to which there could be no learning with no reinforcement[39]. The most important finding in this experiment had to do with a third group, which received no reward on the first 10 trials, and then was suddenly rewarded on Trial 11 (condition NR-R). Group NR-R, on just one trial, shifted from behaving like group NR, to behaving like group R. The implications of this finding are important. First, these results indicate that rats in group NR-R had been learning about the maze even in the absence of reward. Otherwise, how could they perform so well upon receiving the first reward? Second, the reward did not seem to be relevant in learning, but it was necessary in order for learning to be translated into behavior, that is, for *performance*. Thus, the reward provided the rat with the motivation to produce the responses that were necessary

---

[37] Tolman (1932). Because of this, his work is also known as *purposive behaviorism*.

[38] Tolman and Honzik (1930).

[39] Note the difference of terms. Although *reward* and *reinforcer* are interchangeable terms for many, behaviorists prefer the term *reinforcer*. A reinforcer, after all, is a reward that proves effective to strengthen behavior.

to reach the goal location, but the rat had already learned many details about its mazy environment. Because this learning was not apparent until the reward was introduced, it was referred to as *latent learning*[40]. And, because there can be learning without necessarily being expressed into behavior, this study called for a distinction between learning and performance.

Another important implication of the finding of latent learning, or learning in the absence of reward/reinforcement, is that this kind of learning cannot be easily explained from an S-R account. Rather, what the unrewarded rats apparently learned was a set of associations among stimuli in their environment, which were then expressed into behavior when the reward provided the motivation to do so. Accordingly, Tolman proposed an alternative account of learning which he used to call *learning of expectancies*[41], now commonly known as S-S learning. This S-S learning is the basis for the formation of the cognitive map, which is no more than a complex set of expectancies among the many stimuli in the maze. Simply put, in Tolman's framework, what the rat learned in the maze was better described as "at the end of this alley, if you turn right, you will get to the black corridor that leads to food" instead of "at the end of the alley, turn right, then go straight, then eat food".

The use of intervening variables to explain behavior, especially cognitive variables such as expectancies organized in a cognitive map, together with the learning-performance distinction encouraged by the discovery of latent learning sets the point that, in the opinion of many psychologists, marks the origin of cognitive psychology. It can thus be claimed that the cognitive rat was born at the University of California, Berkeley, in Tolman's laboratory. The

---

[40] Or *silent learning* (Dickinson, 1980).

[41] Tolman (1932).

rat would no longer be seen as a simple, mechanistic animal. Or would it?

STUCK IN THE PAST: THE BEHAVIORIST AND THE C-WORD

Skinner died on August 18, 1990, at the age of 86. As of August 17, 1990, he was still actively working. In fact, the evening before his death he completed one of his many rebuttals against cognitive psychology. In his paper, he blamed cognitive psychology for the failure of behavior analysis to receive more attention in psychology. As he stated, behavior analysis had been neglected because "its field had been occupied for so long by that extraordinarily intriguing theory of an internal originating mind or self"[42].

He claimed that human beings have always explained behavior alluding to internal causes, and that (unfortunately) psychology was no exception. Since the times of the Greeks, when psychology was born in its philosophical version (the term *psychology* comes from the Greek *rational study of the soul*), explaining human behavior as arising from private events (ideas, knowledge, emotions, feelings, motivations...) has been commonplace. This was precisely the reason why introspection was used in psychological research as an attempt to dig into the contents of the mind until Watson's behaviorist manifesto declared it a dead-end street. For Skinner, modern cognitive psychology was not much different from the introspective psychology of the last decades of the 19th century because "the problem [is] not introspection ... it [is] the initiating self or mind to which introspection seemed to gain access"[43].

---

[42] Skinner (1990), p. 1209.

[43] Ibid, p. 1209.

In another paper published three years earlier, Skinner had even stronger words against cognitive psychology (as well as against humanistic psychology and psychotherapy). In that paper, Skinner claimed that cognitive psychology was responsible for "unfortunate effects upon psychology as a science"[44] and that "the cognitive restoration of the royal House of Mind [has] worked against the definition of psychology as the science of behavior"[45]. In his opinion, the solution was obvious: "Psychology should confine itself to its accessible subject matter and leave the rest of the story of human behavior to physiology."[46] Although his pugilistic style might be a bit extreme (after all, Skinner's behaviorism was called *radical* for a reason), one cannot help but understand his frustration. As a scientist who devoted a great part of his time to advocate for psychology as serious and respected science, the success of cognitive psychology over behavior analysis was a threat to everything he had worked for in his life. Skinner wanted to see psychology recognized as a natural science (like biology, chemistry, or physics – also known as the *hard* sciences), instead of a social science (like anthropology, linguistics, or education – also known as the *soft* sciences), and the behaviorist approach he proposed met the conditions in order for psychology to achieve such "higher" status. With the return of the mind into psychology, his dream of establishing a new psychology as the science of behavior was over.

Today's cognitive psychology has joined forces with neuroscience and is providing us with the greatest insights into the workings of our brain. Neuroimaging techniques such as fMRI (functional magnetic resonance imaging) now allows us, literally speaking, to see the brain in action. In an fMRI, different colors appear on a computer screen indicating what exact brain structures

---

[44] Skinner (1987), p. 780.

[45] Ibid, p. 784.

[46] Ibid, p. 785.

are activated (and how much) during the performance of different tasks. With such a technique, neuroscientists are not only confirming what previous invasive surgical procedures had already demonstrated (say, that visual information is processed in the occipital lobe), but also providing previously unthinkable information. Now we are starting to ask questions that are everything but ordinary, such as *where does moral judgment take place in our brain?*[47] or *can a whistle traditionally used for long-distance communication activate brain structures be related to spoken-language?*[48]. Thanks to studies like these, cognitive psychology has better health today than ever before. Alas, this is a cognitive psychology that Skinner never met, because the first study using the fMRI[49] was published just one year after his death.

We can only speculate about whether Skinner would change his mind (or, better said, his *verbal behavior*) regarding cognitive psychology if he was still among us today. But chances are that he would still insist on attacking it in yet another paper. In fact, he would point out that what these studies prove is the weakness of cognitive science, which needs neuroscience to do its job. There is no need to speculate about this, for he already stated it in slightly different words: "But psychology may find it dangerous to turn to neurology for help. Once you tell the world that another science will explain what your key terms really mean, you must forgive the world if it decides that the other science is doing the important work"[50].

Today, cognitive psychology is still under attack by some

---

[47] Greene and Haidt (2002).

[48] Carreiras, Lopez, Rivero, and Corina (2005).

[49] Belliveau, Kennedy, McKinstry, Buchbinder, Weisskoff, Cohen, Vevea, Brady, and Rosen (1991).

[50] Skinner (1987), p. 784.

followers of Skinner's ideas (some even call themselves *Skinnerians*). They still refer to the mind as a *black box* and refuse to speak of "cognition" (their own unnamable *c-word*) as a determinant of behavior. Like Skinner, they ignore the fact that cognitive psychology has built itself to be a serious science that, besides sharing the mind as the object of study, has nothing to do regarding its research methods with the introspective psychology of the late 1800s. Let us consider one of the recursive critiques made by Skinnerians about cognitive theories, namely, that they fall in the *homunculus fallacy*. Consider a theory that explains operant behavior, not just in terms of its functional relationship with its consequences and antecedent stimuli, but also in terms of *decision making*. In this theory, multiple responses in a given situation are evaluated first by making hypotheses about their most likely consequences. The Skinnerian psychologist would say that not only the theoretical construct *decision making* is not necessary for explaining behavior, but it also demands an explanation itself. Claiming that we made a decision and responded accordingly is like claiming that a little version of ourselves, a little man (homunculus) that resides in our heads drives our behavior. This little man's behavior (making decisions) must therefore be explained. But how? Maybe there is an even smaller man inside him? This would certainly lead us to an infinite regress *ad absurdum*[51].

It would certainly be a blatant mistake if cognitive psychology made use of little men in its theories to explain human behavior, for the same reasons it would be a huge mistake for biologists to explain our existence on this planet by recurring to the intervention of an alien civilization or a deity. But cognitive psychologists know better than that. The processes they propose are simple processes that, in turn, can be composed of even simpler processes, which are made of even simpler processes... until the processes can no longer

---

[51] As claimed by Ryle (1949/2002).

be further broken down. Each of these extremely simple processes performs a specific operation in an automatic manner. Individually, each process is not intelligent, but when many simple processes are organized in a coherent system, they produce intelligence. This is what Minsky[52] called the *society of mind*, and what Lindsay and Norman[53] called a *pandemonium* (their pattern-recognition system was composed of little demons[54] that completed specific successive tasks of growing complexity).

In this debate between Skinnerian and cognitive psychologists[55], those who study animal cognition find themselves in a cross fire. This is especially true for psychologists working with rats or pigeons. On one hand, their research is performed with a methodology mostly shaped by Skinner's tradition (the procedures of operant conditioning and the experimental apparatuses are Skinner's legacy). On the other hand, although they make good use of learning theory, their agenda does not include demonstrating lawful relationships between stimuli and responses or between responses and its consequences. Rather, they are interested in understanding how the animal's mind works. That is, they are cognitive psychologists using Skinnearian tools in their research. They dwell in between two paradigms, and are strangers to both. But they also have the best of both worlds: a wonderful object of research (the animal mind) and a powerful set of theories and methods (learning theory) to study it. The beauty of this science lies in the awe-inspiring findings that it has produced.

---

[52] Minsky (1985).

[53] Lindsay and Norman (1972), after Selfridge (1959).

[54] Of course, the little demons were figurative. But their choice of demons to represent psychological processes makes perfect sense when considering that the symbol of psychology is ψ (psi), the first letter in the Greek word *psyche* (ψυχή), and that this symbol resembles a trident.

[55] Skinnearians have also been attacked by pugilistic cognitive psychologists on the nativist tradition such as Chomsky or Pinker, to cite just two.

CHAPTER 3: LEARNING SPICED WITH COGNITION

Loosely defined, *learning* consists of being able to change or adapt behavior according to experiences with the environment. It could be said that learning processes have arisen evolutionarily as a necessary consequence of environmental complexity and change. An animal species living in a simple and easily predictable environment would be better off by relying upon innate, fixed behaviors. For this species, specific reactions to discrete stimuli would suffice. Although coming to this world with a package of "instructions" to deal with every possible situation does not necessarily make the task of survival easier, this "strategy" is certainly adaptive, for it is both advantageous (since day one, all individuals have the potential to perform effective behaviors in any possible situation) and economical (it allows the individuals to bypass the learning process altogether and devote resources to other tasks). But we, humans, live in environments that are everything but simple and stationary. Our physical and social contexts are so intricate that no innate package of "directives" would be accurate and comprehensive enough to guide us through every possible situation. Furthermore, given that we live in a rapidly changing environment, innate "guidelines" are likely to be outdated and, thus, useless even before we ever have a chance to "unwrap the instruction manual". For us, a handful of simple reflexive behaviors (for example, sucking, crying, startle, etc.), along with a tremendously powerful learning machinery, provides a much better solution.

Learning is not an exclusively human ability; rather, this ability is present to some extent across the animal kingdom. The question, of course, is how much of a given species' behavior is controlled by its genes and how much is the product of experience.

This leads to the old *nature versus nurture* debate that was held by scientists in different areas, psychology included, over the last decades. With the reader's permission, I will tiptoe around this debate. At least in psychology, it was resolved long ago, with the common-sense acceptance of the combined contribution of both nature and nurture in the production of behavior; that is, behavior is the result of complex interactions between genetic and experiential factors. We must keep in mind that this book is concerned with animal behavior and, more precisely, with the behavior of the *par excellence* animal of the psychology laboratory – the rat. Therefore, it might be more useful to frame the question in terms of comparative psychology and ask, instead, what do studies on animal learning tell us about the rat's (and other animals') ability to adapt its behavior as a function of experience.

The times of the Cartesian dualism, which portrayed nonhuman animals as mere automata that mechanistically reacted to their environment based on very simple reflexes, are long gone[1]. We have also overcome the resolution of this dualism provided by the radical behaviorist, which admittedly gave some credit to nonhuman animals (after all, they were used in learning experiments for a reason), but took the mind away from us (at least, Descartes credited us for having one) and reduced humans to a more elaborate version of the laboratory rat. We now think of animal behavior as sustained by cognitive processes that might well be comparable to our own. This makes perfect sense within the Darwinian theory of evolution[2]: to the extent that we share common (extinct) ancestors with other species, those traits (physical and psychological) that were already present in the common ancestor have a chance to be retained in living species that evolved

---

[1] At least in science. Unfortunately, this notion still prevails in some variations of *pop psychology*.

[2] See Chapter 6 for a discussion of this theory in regards to animal cognition.

from this ancestor (a primitive character). Our cognitive processes (or, more precisely, the *building blocks* of our cognitive processes), therefore, rather than being exclusively human, might instead be deeply rooted in the phylogenetic tree.

In this chapter I discuss the experimental evidence that supports the view that information processing in humans, at least at a very basic level, does not greatly differ from the way information is processed by rats and other animals. First, I will examine the kind of information we typically extract from an animal conditioning experiment in order to draw our conclusions as well as what might be the "boldest" assumption in our approach, namely, that animals might form (and efficiently use) mental representations of events. Then, I will peruse some studies that show how strong the parallel is between human learning and animal (rat) conditioning results.

WHAT DO WE SEEK IN AN ANIMAL CONDITIONING EXPERIMENT?

The experiment is, no doubt, the "backbone" of the scientific method. For a scientist, the experiment comes as a natural consequence of considering the current evidence and its several interpretations (or theories) to, then, further ask "what if..." questions (or hypotheses). Competing theories will make different predictions about the outcome of a certain event; and the argument among theories will not be won on the ground of logic or rhetoric (as is the case in philosophy), but in the laboratory. In the end, it is the cold, hard data what determines which theory is right and which theory is wrong. Being a good scientist, thus, requires not only extreme curiosity, but also a humble approach to the pursuit of knowledge. The experiment is the scientist's ultimate reality check or, in other words, what keeps our feet on the ground. Like any other reality check, it will sometimes hurt (a much cherished theory can fall down like a house of cards with a tiny blow). Nevertheless, the experiment will eventually provide the stubborn scientist with one of the most gratifying experiences on Earth: the pleasure of having grasped the workings of our world or, at least, a tiny parcel thereof. Famous physicist Leo Kadanoff put this feeling in to near-perfect words.

> *It's an experience like no other experience I can describe, the best thing that can happen to a scientist, realizing that something that's happened in his or her mind exactly corresponds to something that happens in nature. It's startling every time it occurs. One is surprised that a construct of one's own mind can actually be realized in the honest-to-goodness world out there. A great shock, and a great, great joy.*[3]

If the experiment is what connects the scientist's mind with the "honest-to-goodness world out there", it is fair to say that the animal learning experiment provides a special kind of connection between the scientist's mind and the laboratory animal's mind.

As any other experiment, the animal conditioning experiment consists of systematically manipulating one or more variables (independent variables) and registering and measuring one or more variables (dependent variables), while diligently (or even obsessively) keeping all other things constant. In an animal conditioning experiment, the independent variables usually consist of stimuli that are presented to the animals, such as a light, a noise, a flavored solution, food or water, or a mild electric shock. The dependent variables are the animals' responses to the stimuli they are given. Typical responses that can be recorded in a Skinner box include lever pressing, head entries to the magazine or food hopper (a little aperture in which food can be delivered), nose pokes (inserting the nose in one of several apertures), licks from a bottle spout, freezing (an almost complete absence of body movement), and startle (a sudden movement). With some exceptions, the

---

[3] Quote borrowed from Gleick (1987), p. 189.

experimenter rarely considers these stimuli and responses important on their own; rather, what matters are the functional relationships among stimuli and responses. Stimuli are used to provide the animal with an experience, a piece of information to be learned, and responses are used to assess such learning. Responses are the tools that allow us a peek into the animal's mind[4].

As I discussed in Chapter 2, the science of animal learning and behavior is rooted in the traditions of Pavlov and Watson (classical or Pavlovian or respondent conditioning) and of Thorndike and Skinner (instrumental or operant conditioning). For some researchers, the classical-operant distinction does matter. In fact, many devote their whole lives to exclusively conduct research within one of these paradigms. This is especially true for those who conduct animal learning studies with no direct interest in animal learning *per se*, but as a means to achieve another goal, say, to develop effective human behavior modification techniques (here the operant conditioning paradigm is typically preferred) or to understand the neural substrates of learning (behavioral neuroscience, in which both classical and operant conditioning paradigms are great contributors, but which seems to prefer the classical conditioning paradigm). For those with an interest in animal learning and behavior, an animal conditioning experiment may be conducted within either paradigm and still provide comparable information. After all, these two paradigms involve lawful relationships among stimuli and responses. In other words, they both comprise associative learning processes and the laws governing these processes are presumed to be the same across learning systems and animal species.

The previous statement can be questionable (and I am pretty sure that some of my colleagues would not endorse it), but it helps

---

[4] This statement is nothing but heretic from the radical behaviorist's viewpoint. I will discuss its implications in the next section.

me to make my point clear: to the current animal learning researcher, classical and operant responses (for example, the number of drops of saliva and lever presses, respectively) are just the overt behavioral expression of an underlying psychological process, namely, the formation of an association or link between two events (stimuli and/or responses). To the extent that one can measure the strength (frequency, intensity, latency, duration, etc.) of this behavior, the strength of the underlying association that produces it can also be inferred. But this necessarily takes us to another topic, that is, the presumed existence of *mental representations* in nonhuman animals.

A CANDLE IN THE "BLACK BOX": MENTAL REPRESENTATIONS IN ANIMAL LEARNING

In Chapter 2, I discussed the origins of the stimulus-response (S-R) and stimulus-stimulus (S-S) theories of learning, but I did not fully consider the implications of these two views. These two theories (or, better said, *families* of theories) might often be able to explain the same experimental evidence, but they do it in subtle, yet radically different ways. It is no exaggeration to state that, for once, thinking of animal learning from one viewpoint or the other is more than just adopting a theoretical approach. It is adopting a whole philosophy of animal intelligence.

An example will help us better understand the main differences between the S-R and S-S approaches. Let us assume that one group of hungry animals, which we will call Paired, receives an experimental treatment consisting of 20 pairings of a 30-second tone with two small pellets of food. Another group of animals, which we will call Unpaired, receives the same number of presentations of the tone and the food, but with a critical difference: these presentations are unpaired (given separately). Over the treatment, the animals in Group Paired, but not those in Group

Unpaired, start making new responses. When the tone is presented, the animals in Group Paired run to the food magazine, where they occasionally insert their heads prior to food delivery. Moreover, as treatment progresses this behavior gains strength for Group Paired, occurring more readily after the tone onset, with a higher frequency, and for a longer time.

What can we conclude from these results? We could infer that hungry rats learn to make a new response (magazine entries) when they are presented with an auditory stimulus (the tone) together with a motivationally-relevant stimulus (food pellets). We could also infer that temporal contiguity (that is, closeness in time) is a critical factor in order for this learning to take place, given that this new behavior was found in Group Paired, but not in Group Unpaired. In other words, we could infer that the pairing of the tone with food caused the tone to elicit a conditioned response (or CR) that it did not elicit prior to the treatment. That is, the tone has become a conditioned stimulus (or CS) and now triggers this conditioned response, along with others (for example, salivation, head-jerking), which are of adaptive value to the animal because they maximize exposure to and ingestion of food. At this point, we have a great story to tell from our experiment. In fact, this is the story one would expect to be told from the S-R viewpoint. But, is it good enough?

We could still push the interpretation of our results a little further and say that the tone elicits these behaviors in Group Paired (but not in Group Unpaired) because it allows the animals in this group to *predict* the imminent presentation of food. We could state that the animals have formed mental representations of the tone and the food, as well as an association between the tone and the food representations and, as a consequence, the presentation of the tone elicits an *expectation* of food. Because of this expectation of food, the animals run to the magazine, where they wait for the food to be delivered. And, finally, the cherry on top of the cake: we can also assume that the strength of the observed behavior/s directly correlates with the strength of the underlying expectation of food. That is, the faster the animals in Group Paired run to the magazine, the more times and/or the longer they keep their heads in the magazine, the more strongly they expect food to be presented in the magazine. In other words, the strength of the animals' observable behavior in the presence of the tone presumably serves as an indicator of the strength of the underlying tone-food association.

EVIDENCE OF MENTAL REPRESENTATIONS IN THE RAT

We have seen that animal behavior can be explained from a purely behavioral and mechanistic view (S-R theories) and a more cognitive or mentalistic perspective (S-S theories). But, which approach should we adopt? Certainly, explaining animal behavior in terms of mental representations sounds fancier than doing so based on automatic responses to stimuli, but admittedly this is a pretty lame reason to pick sides. In fact, if both S-R and S-S theories explain exactly the same amount of experimental evidence, one should adopt the S-R theory for a simple reason: S-R theories are more parsimonious, that is, they explain the same amount of evidence by making fewer assumptions and, hence, in a simpler manner. That is, the S-R view should be the theory of choice *by default*, unless it was seriously challenged by evidence requiring the mediating role of mental representations in order to be explained.

As a matter of fact, such evidence exists, and in studies using rats perhaps its best example comes from experiments using a technique known as *US devaluation*[5]. Devaluing the US merely consists of reducing its value to the animal, something that can be achieved in multiple manners. For example, a food US can be devalued by pairing it with an aversive or noxious event such as the

---

[5] Research using this technique is quite extensive, but a good example can be found in Holland and Rescorla (1975).

injection of an emetic (for example, lithium chloride, or LiCl), X-rays, or exposure to high-speed rotation[6]. Or, alternatively, the value of a food US can be reduced by granting the animals free access to food (food has a lower value for a satiated than for a hungry animal). The basic US-devaluation treatment is depicted in the following figure.

Graphical representation of the associations learned by a rat in a US-devaluation experiment. In a first stage, a neutral stimulus (for example, a light) is paired with a biologically significant stimulus or US (for example, food). After several of these pairings, the light becomes a CS that elicits appetitive conditioned responses (for example, salivation, magazine entries, or sign tracking). Then, in a second stage, the food US is paired with a noxious event, such as the poisoning caused by an injection of LiCl. At test, the presentation of the light does no longer evoke appetitive responses; if anything, aversive responses are elicited.

The application of the US-devaluation technique to ascertain if classical conditioning involves the action of mental representations (S-S theories) and not just stimuli triggering automatic responses (S-R) is quite straightforward. After the

---

[6] This sort of "experimental illness", as harsh as it might sound, is not unlike the illness normally experienced by animals in the wild. For example, the ingestion of certain foods containing natural toxins might cause illness (sometimes it can even be fatal), a scenario that resembles LiCl-induced illness in these experiments (with the difference that, in the laboratory, the doses of LiCl are carefully prepared and very rarely result in accidental death).

animals receive enough pairings of the CS (for example, a tone) with the food US, and a strong and stable appetitive conditioned response is elicited by the CS, the US is devalued for some subjects (Group Dev), but not for others (Group NoDev). Obviously, consumption of the food US should decrease for Group Dev, but not for Group NoDev. Be it because the food US was paired with a noxious event or just because the animals in this group are satiated, consumption of the food US will decline for Group Dev. But, the critical question is: will Group Dev continue responding to the tone CS that was previously paired with the food US?

According to the S-R viewpoint, these animals should still produce strong appetitive conditioned responses in the presence of the tone, even though the food US was previously devalued. According to the S-R theories, the CS directly elicits the conditioned response and, thus, any treatment involving the US that is performed after the CS-US pairings (that is, once the CS produces conditioned responding) should not affect the conditioned response. In other words, the S-R viewpoint counterintuitively predicts that, in Group Dev, the tone CS that was previously paired with the food US will continue eliciting responses such as salivation and/or head entries in the magazine following the US-devaluation treatment, even when the food is no longer appealing to these animals.

Things are quite different from the S-S standpoint. According to this set of theories, during the pairings of the tone with the food, an association is formed between the mental representations of these events. Hence, the presentation of the tone activates the representation of the food US. In other words, the tone makes the animal think of the food US. The conditioned response is the consequence of the activation of the food US representation by the tone CS. This response allows the animal to get ready for the occurrence of the US (the delivery of food, in this case). In the S-S framework, devaluing the US following the CS-US pairings should therefore decrease conditioned responding to the CS. For the animals in Group Dev, now the presentation of the tone CS activates the representation of a food US that is either "yucky" (when the US was paired with an aversive event) or simply not very appealing (when the animals are no longer hungry) at the time of testing. Should these animals respond to the CS as they did prior to the US-devaluation treatment? According to the S-S view, they should not... and this is exactly what many studies have found[7].

The technique described above has also been employed to study whether, in operant conditioning, animals form a mental representation of the outcome or reinforcer. That is, in the three-term contingency of operant conditioning (stimulus-response-outcome, or S-R-O), do animals learn something about the outcome itself? This question might seem ludicrous, given that now operant conditioning is generally viewed as due, in part, to the formation of an association between the operant response and the outcome (R-O). For example, it is broadly accepted that the reason why the rat presses the lever in the Skinner box is that it has learned that lever presses yield food. Current views notwithstanding, the outcome did not receive such special treatment in traditional accounts. Admittedly, it always played a critical role in operant learning (it served to stamp in the S-R association in Thorndike's Law of Effect or to strengthen or reinforce the operant response in Skinner's view), but it never was something special enough for the animal to learn about.

So where is the evidence of R-O associations in operant conditioning? In a brilliant experiment[8], two operant responses (pushing a vertical rod either to the left or to the right) were followed by different outcomes (food pellets or sucrose). That is, for half of the animals, pushing the lever to the left would yield

---

[7] For a representative study, see Holland and Rescorla (1975).

[8] Colwill and Rescorla (1986).

food pellets and pushing it to the right would yield sucrose; whereas for the other half these relationships were reversed (pushing the lever to the left would yield sucrose and pushing it to the right would yield food pellets). Once both operant responses were frequently produced, the *outcome devaluation* treatment was carried out. In this phase, the operant responses were not possible (the rod had been removed), and one of the outcomes (food pellets for half of the animals and sucrose for the other half) was freely presented, followed by an injection of LiCl. Thus, after this session, one of the outcomes had completely lost its appeal for the animals (it was actually quite "yucky"). At test, the vertical rod was reintroduced and the animals could freely produce any of the responses, that is, push the rod to the left or to the right. Interestingly, the rats mostly made the response that produced the non-devalued outcome. In other words, they stopped working for the outcome that had been devalued. This makes perfect sense: why else would one work for something "yucky", when that effort could be put into getting something that is still tasty? The evidence of outcome representations in operant conditioning is compelling. After all, operant conditioning is also known as *goal-directed action*[9] for a reason: the operant response is produced with the intention of achieving a goal, that is, obtaining the outcome.

Devaluing the US or outcome following the CS-US or R-O pairings is not the only available technique to study the role of mental representations in Pavlovian and operant conditioning. A few years before the aforementioned experiments on US/outcome devaluation were performed, an old procedure known as *sensory preconditioning*[10] had been resuscitated to answer very similar questions. In a typical sensory preconditioning treatment[11], the

---

[9] See Dickinson and Balleine (1994).

[10] See Brodgen (1939).

[11] See Experiment 4 of Rizley and Rescorla (1972). Also see Rescorla and Cunningham
(Footnote continued on next page)

animal first receives pairings of two neutral stimuli, that is, stimuli
that evoke no discrete response (other than an attentional orienting
response, or the orientation of the sense organs to the source of
stimulation), such as pairings of a light stimulus with a tone
stimulus. Then, in a second phase, the tone stimulus is paired with a
biologically significant stimulus or US, such as a footshock. At
testing, a conditioned response (conditioned fear, in the present
example) is observed when the light stimulus is presented alone,
relative to control conditions lacking either the light-tone pairings
or the tone-footshock pairings. This is summarized in the following
figure.

Graphical representation of the associations learned by a rat in a sensory
preconditioning experiment. In the first stage, a neutral stimulus (for
example, a light) is paired with another neutral stimulus (for example, a
tone). Then, in the second phase, the tone is paired with a biologically
significant stimulus or US (for example, a footshock). At test, the
presentation of the light evokes a fear conditioned response.

These results are interesting for two reasons. First, the light is
never paired directly with the footshock US, but with the tone,
which in turn is paired with the footshock US. Still, the light elicits a
fear response when presented at test. And, second, the tone is a

___

(1978), and Rescorla and Freberg (1978), for representative experiments involving flavor-
flavor associations.

neutral stimulus during its pairings with the light in the first phase. This second feature of the sensory preconditioning procedure is critical because it precludes an explanation of the results based on the acquisition of an S-R association. Because both the light and the tone were neutral stimuli during their initial pairings, and because the light only came to elicit a fear conditioned response after the tone had been paired with the footshock US, this effect can only be explained by assuming that an association was formed between the mental representations of the light stimulus and the tone stimulus which, in turn, got associated with the footshock stimulus. Simply put, based on these associations, the tone presentation makes the rat think of the tone which, in turn, makes the rat expect the occurrence of footshock, thereby triggering a conditioned fear response. That is, this phenomenon can only be accounted for by the S-S viewpoint.

The sensory preconditioning effect is related to two other phenomena. One is the previously discussed US-devaluation effect, in which a neutral stimulus (for example, a light) was first paired with food, which was then paired with a noxious event, such as LiCl. If we ignore the differences in the specific kind of stimuli (and their biological significance) employed in each procedure, one can see that both cases involve the acquisition of two associations, one between Events A and B (light-food or light-tone) and one between Events B and C (food-LiCl or tone-shock). The response elicited by Event A at test could only be explained based on the integration of these two associations in memory, resulting in an A-B-C link[12].

The other related effect basically consists of the reversal of the treatment phases given in the sensory preconditioning procedure. In this effect, known as *second-order conditioning*[13], the tone-

---

[12] This integration of the A-B and B-C links into an A-B-C link can also be seen as obeying the rule of transitivity in mathematics and logic.

[13] Pavlov (1927).

footshock pairings are given first, followed by the light-tone pairings. Based on the previous discussion, one can appreciate that, in spite of their apparent similarity, an important difference emerges: contrary to what happens in sensory preconditioning, in second-order conditioning the tone is not a neutral stimulus, but a (fear evoking) CS, during the light-tone pairings. Therefore, contrary to sensory preconditioning (which can only be explained from an S-S viewpoint), second-order conditioning can also be explained from a traditional S-R account. In order to do so, this account would merely need to assume that, during the light-tone pairings, the light entered into an association with the conditioned response elicited by the tone (due to the tone's prior pairings with the US). In fact, many studies[14] have demonstrated that, when it comes to second-order conditioning, the S-R account seems to fit better with evidence than the S-S account.

We are, thus, left with two highly related effects that only differ in the order in which the treatment phases are given, one of them explainable only from the S-S viewpoint (sensory preconditioning) and the other explainable from either S-S or S-R viewpoints (second-order conditioning). Simple logic says that the common mechanism to both effects, namely, S-S learning, should be the mechanism operating in second-order conditioning. But evidence defies logic, showing that S-S and S-R accounts of learning are perfectly compatible from the animal's point of view. We, the scientists, strive to find the most parsimonious explanation for the results we harvest in our laboratory, but simplicity is not always in the animals' agenda. Why should an organism need to choose between two mechanisms when each of them might yield exclusive advantages? There is no need to choose indeed. The point here is not to disprove the existence of an S-R learning mechanism, but to make a stand for the existence of an S-S mechanism and, thus, the

---

[14] See Rizley and Rescorla (1972), and Holland and Rescorla (1975).

important role of mental representations in animal conditioning paradigms, which are traditionally dominated by the mechanistic viewpoint of the S-R theories.

One last phenomenon deserves to be briefly discussed in this section, for it provides straightforward evidence of the formation and use of stimulus representations by rats (and other animals) in conditioning preparations. This effect is known as *mediated conditioning*[15] and, as its name suggests, it consists of conditioning a response to a CS in an indirect or mediated manner. The basic procedure in a mediated conditioning experiment consists of pairings of a neutral stimulus (for example, a tone) with a biologically significant stimulus (for example, food US), followed by pairings of the tone with a noxious event (for example, a LiCl injection). This is illustrated in the following figure.

Graphical representation of the associations learned by a rat in a mediated conditioning experiment. In the first stage, a neutral stimulus (for example, a tone) is paired with a biologically significant stimulus or US (for example, food). Then, in the second stage, the tone is paired with a noxious event, such as the illness caused by an injection of LiCl. At test, the food US is poorly consumed.

In this procedure the target stimulus is the food US. When

---

[15] See Holland (1981).

food is presented at test, it is poorly consumed by the animals. In fact, the animals react to the food with aversive responses (for example, conditioned nausea), almost as if the food itself had been paired with illness, something that never happened. But, if we carefully think about it, maybe the food was actually paired with the illness – only in the animal's mind. The explanation of this effect is strikingly simple. On each tone-LiCl pairing, the tone evokes the memory of food (based on the previous tone-food pairings) which, in turn, becomes associated with illness. Let us put it in a slightly different way: presenting an associate of the food (the tone) has an effect that is comparable to presenting the food itself. Obviously, the mental representations of food elicited by the tone and the physical presentation of real food will differ in terms of richness, accuracy, and vividness. Still, the activation of the mental representation of food seems to work in a similar way regardless of whether it belongs to the realm of "normal perception" or to that of "hallucination". Mental imagery can expand our ability to form adaptive associations, but only when its elements are lawfully linked to environmental stimuli. Like us, rats seem to be able to exploit the power of imagery without losing touch with reality.

KEEP IT REAL

The activation of the mental representation of a stimulus (for example, food) by the presentation of another stimulus (for example, a tone) might involve not only the expectation of the occurrence of food, but also the mental recreation of the food stimulus (what we normally refer to as *remembering*, a reality-based form of mental imagery). As previously mentioned, mental imagery can greatly expand the potential of associative learning, but only provided that it does not lose touch with the real world. It makes sense, therefore, that animals should make an effort to constantly contrast their expectations with reality. In other words, animals should compare whatever was expected to happen with whatever actually happened.

In a recently published study[16], rats received a sensory preconditioning treatment consisting of tone-light pairings in a first phase, followed by light-sucrose pairings in a second phase. At test, the tone was presented alone. Importantly, for one condition, the light bulb that previously provided the light stimulus remained in place (but unlit) whereas for another condition it was removed from the chamber and replaced with a blank aluminum plate. Why was this simple manipulation so important? Remember that sensory preconditioning presumably occurs due to the activation of mental representations of absent stimuli. Specifically, in this study, the tone presumably activated a mental representation of the light which, in turn, would then activate the representation of sucrose. But keep in mind that, at test, the tone is presented alone and that this is totally unexpected, since the tone was always followed by the light during training. Should the unexpected omission of the light after the tone somehow disrupt the expectation of sucrose as well? The answer to this question is *yes*, but only if the rat could determine with certainty that, in fact, the light did not occur.

Here is where the critical manipulation of this study, namely, whether the light bulb remained in place or was removed during testing, plays its role. In the condition with the light bulb available (but unlit), the rats could determine the omission of the light stimulus, whereas in the condition for which the light bulb had been removed from the chamber this simply was not possible. Knowing that the light did not occur is not the same as not knowing whether the light occurred. Accordingly, this study found that the tone elicited conditioned responses (nose pokes) indicative of an expectation of sucrose in the condition lacking the light bulb at test, but not in the condition for which the light bulb was still in

---

[16] Blaisdell, Leising, Stahlman, and Waldmann (2009).

place. That is, when the presence of the unlit light bulb made it clear that the expected light stimulus was not occurring, the rats did not even bother to check for sucrose. This result once again reinforces the idea that functional mental imagery, as important as it might be, cannot be detached from reality.

RAT, THE STATISTICIAN

The previous section addressed an important question about animal learning, namely, what is learned in classical and instrumental conditioning paradigms? Is it an automatic S-R link or a richer, more sophisticated S-S (or R-O) link involving mental representations of the events? Another, more basic question might be asked as well: how does an animal learn to associate these events or, in other words, what are the necessary conditions of associative learning?

To begin with, the events must co-occur in space and time. That is, they must be *contiguous*. In animal experiments, such contiguity can always be guaranteed. Pressing a lever immediately yields a food pellet, pecking on an illuminated key delivers a grain food with no delay, and a tone always ends with a footshock. A learning system that relies on the contiguous occurrence of events as a condition to associate the events can be said to be adapted to reality. In spite of the complicated causal texture of our world, many relationships among separate events can be easily pinpointed merely based on their joint spatiotemporal occurrence. For example, placing your hand on a hot surface results in immediate pain, a train in the Subway is closely preceded by its noise, a vending machine delivers a can of soda as soon as you insert the money and make a selection, and the sight and smell of the food on your plate closely precede its taste. To better understand the critical role played by contiguity in the learning of associations between the previous pairs of events, try to imagine what would happen if placing your hand on a hot surface did not cause pain right away, but minutes (or even seconds) later. Or if you could hear the noise of the train, but the train never came. Or if the vending machine delivered the can of soda hours after you pressed the key. Or if you could see and smell the food, but failed to taste it in your mouth right away. Clearly, contiguity is a necessary condition to learn an association between two events. The alternative, learning an association between non-contiguous events, certainly makes no sense. Consider the potentially infinite number of non-contiguous events that could be happening over the course of a single day. Contiguity helps you narrow the list of things you might want to consider putting together in your mind.

First acknowledged by the Greek philosopher Aristotle[17], the importance of contiguity in associative learning survived the scrutiny, two millennia later, of British empiricists such as Thomas Brown, Thomas Hobbes, David Hume, John Locke, and John Stuart Mill. In their search for the rules of association among the sensations and ideas responsible for filling what Locke called the *tabula rasa* (blank slate), these philosophers agreed that, out of Aristotle's three laws of association (contiguity, similarity, and contrast), contiguity was central to the building of the contents of the mind[18]. Other important rules were also proposed. For example, Thomas Brown suggested to take into account how frequently and how recently the associations co-occurred. David Hume also adopted Aristotle's similarity (resemblance), while adding the important distinction between cause and effect.

The early scientific study of behavior also relied upon the assumption that contiguity was a necessary condition for the classical or instrumental conditioning of new responses. In fact, contiguity was believed to be not only a necessary condition, but

---

[17] In his *De memoria et reminiscentia*.

[18] Contrary to the laws of contiguity and similarity, the law of contrast has not received much empirical support.

also a sufficient one. That is, the contiguous presentation of the CS with the US (Pavlov) or the response with the outcome (Thorndike[19]) was, in itself, enough to guarantee the formation of an association. Interestingly, because repetition of the contiguous presentation of the events resulted in the strengthening of the conditioned response, the very repetition of the co-occurring events (what Thomas Brown referred to as the *frequency* of the co-occurrence of the associations) became synonymous of contiguity. Nowadays, the term *contiguity* is interchangeably used to refer to either the temporal and/or spatial proximity of events (its original meaning) or the frequency of the pairing of two events.

Things, however, are not quite that simple. Contiguity (both in terms of temporal/spatial proximity and of frequency of co-occurrence) might well be a necessary condition for the association of events, but it is far from being a sufficient condition. One also needs to consider the degree to which these two events covary or, in other words, the degree to which the occurrence of one event is lawfully related to the occurrence of the other. Consider the following example. For some reason, every time you press a key on a computer keyboard, your computer beeps and the message "Hello there" appears on the computer screen. You might be prone to believe that you are somehow causing the presentation of the message on your computer screen. But you could be wrong. In order to make sure that pressing a key causes the presentation of the message, you also need to ascertain what happens when you *do not* press the key. If the "Hello there" message appeared if, and only if, you had previously pressed the key, a causal link between your response and the consequence could be posited. If, by contrast, the "Hello there" kept appearing on the screen at a regular rate,

---

[19] As stated in his Law of Effect: "Of several responses made to the same situation, those which are *accompanied or closely followed by* satisfaction to the animal" (italics by the author; from Thorndike, 1911, p. 244).

regardless of whether you had pressed the key... would you not think that something else, perhaps a virus, is causing the presentation of the message on the screen?

The point here is that, in order to assess if your response (pressing the key) is instrumental in producing the outcome (message on the screen), you need to consider not only what happens when you make the response, but also what happens when you do not make it. This comparison between the probability of the occurrence of one event in the presence and in the absence of another event is what is commonly referred to as *contingency*.

ESTIMATING CONTINGENCIES

The contingency existing between two events, Event 1 (E1) and Event 2 (E2), determines to what extent such events co-occur or co-vary[20]. This contingency can be easily calculated by means of a simple statistic, known as ΔP (Delta P)[21], which basically consists of computing the probability of E2 conditional on the previous occurrence of E1 or, in other words, the difference between the probability of the occurrence of E2 in the presence of E1 and the probability of the occurrence of E2 in the absence of E1. This can be formalized with a simple equation: $\Delta P = P(E2|E1) - P(E2|\text{no } E1)$. How can we calculate each of these probabilities in order to estimate the value of ΔP in a given situation? In spite of its intricate appearance, it is quite easy. First, we create a table in which the

---

[20] The term *contingency* is highly related to the more popular term *correlation*. In fact, both statistics indicate a relation between two variables. However, a correlation involves two continuous variables (variables that can adopt any value within a certain range, for example, relations between age and salary, weight and speed, or IQ and academic performance), whereas a contingency involves two dichotomous or binary variables (variables that can only adopt two values, for example, pressing on a button [either you press the button or not] turns the lights on [the lights are either on or off], calling a cab [either you call it or not] makes a cab stop for you [the cab either stops or not]).

[21] See Allan (1980).

presence and absence of E1 (E1 vs. no E1) are combined with the presence and absence of E2 (E2 vs. no E2). This results in what is called a 2 x 2 contingency matrix, like the one depicted below.

	E2	no E2
E1	*a* *fa*	*b* *fb*
no E1	*c* *fc*	*d* *fd*

This matrix contains 4 cells. In each cell, we can register the frequencies of the trials with the different combinations of the presence and the absence of E1 and E2. Specifically, cell *a* corresponds to the frequency of trials with both E1 and E2 present (*fa*); cell *b* corresponds to the frequency of trials with E1 present and E2 absent (*fb*); cell *c* corresponds to the frequency of trials with E1 absent and E2 present (*fc*); and cell *d* corresponds to the frequency of trials with both E1 and E2 absent (*fd*). Once the frequencies (*fa*, *fb*, *fc*, and *fd*) in the 2 x 2 contingency matrix are known, ΔP can be easily calculated as follows: $\Delta P = P(E2|E1) - P(E2|\text{no } E1) = fa/(fa+fb) - fc/(fc+fd)$. Thus, in this equation, the probability of E2 given E1, or $P(E2|E1)$, which is the same as saying *the chance of E2 happening when the presence of E1 is held constant*, equals *fa/(fa+fb)*. Analogously, the probability of E2 in the absence of E1, or $P(E2|\text{no } E1)$, which means *the chance of E2 happening when the absence of E1 is held constant*, equals *fc/(fc+fd)*.

In order to fully understand the great explanatory value of the statistic ΔP, I will play a bit with made-up numbers. But first, there are a few things we need to know. Each of the probabilities in the equation, as in any probability, will consist of a real number ranging between 0 and 1. This means that the value of ΔP will range between +1 and -1, with the final value adopted by ΔP having a specific *psychological* meaning. Simply put, a positive value of ΔP (ΔP > 0) means that the probability of the occurrence of E2 is higher in the presence of E1 than in its absence, which means that E1 maintains a generative (or excitatory) relationship with E2. In other words, when E1 is present, E2 will likely happen too. By contrast, a negative value of ΔP (ΔP < 0), means that the occurrence of E2 is higher in the absence of E1 than in its presence, which means that E1 maintains a preventive (or inhibitory) relationship with E2. In other words, when E1 is present, E2 will be unlikely to occur. Finally, a null value of ΔP (ΔP = 0) means that the occurrence of E2 is completely independent of the occurrence of E1, which means that E1 maintains no relationship whatsoever with E2.

Now, let us play with the numbers. For starters, take the following example. Imagine that you have spent a few days training your dog to come to you on command. Although you have the impression that your training is being effective, you are not fully certain (sometimes she does not seem to get it). In order to ascertain whether your dog has really learned something, you decide to record the number of times she comes to you, both in the presence and absence of your command. This results in the following frequencies:

	E2: Dog comes	no E2: Dog does not come
E1: "Come!" command	*a* 9	*b* 1
no E1: No "Come!" command	*c* 2	*d* 8

Once these numbers are in place, calculating ΔP is pretty simple: ΔP = 9/(9+1) - 2/(2+8) = 0.90 - 0.20 = 0.70. As I previously mentioned, a positive value of ΔP indicates that Event 1 maintains a generative or excitatory relationship with Event 2. Thus, the value of ΔP in the present example, +0.70, clearly confirms your impression: your dog seems to be more likely to come to you when you prompt her, although she is yet to be perfectly trained.

Let us consider another example. Your child seems to be having trouble completing his homework. You guess the problem might have to do with the TV, which is always on while he tries to do his homework. So, you decide to manipulate the availability of the TV during homework time and conduct your assessment with the following 2 x 2 table.

	E2: Homework	no E2: No homework
E1: TV	*a* 0	*b* 7
no E1: No TV	*c* 11	*d* 1

As for the ΔP value: $\Delta P = 0/(0+7) - 11/(11+1) = 0.00 - 0.91 = -0.91$. As I previously mentioned, a negative value of ΔP indicates that Event 1 maintains a preventive or inhibitory relationship with Event 2. This means that the ΔP value, -0.91, confirms your impression: the TV is keeping your child from completing his homework.

Now let us contemplate one final example. After trying a new brand of allergy medicine, you suspect that it is causing you to lose some sleep. You decide to apply your knowledge of ΔP to solve this new mystery. Here are your numbers:

	E2: Insomnia	no E2: No insomnia
E1: Allergy medicine	*a* 4	*b* 1
no E1: No allergy medicine	*c* 5	*d* 1

And this is your resulting ΔP value: $\Delta P = 4/(4+1) - 5/(5+1) = 0.80 - 0.83 = -0.03$. In this case, the value of ΔP, -0.03, does not support your impressions. This allergy medicine cannot be claimed to be responsible for your insomnia. Your false impression might have been due to your having focused exclusively on the incidences of insomnia after taking the medicine (a quite high probability indeed, 0.80), and disregarding the fact that your sleep problems also seemed to occur on nights on which you had taken no medicine (also a high probability, 0.83). As with the example of the "Hello there" message on your computer screen, this example also serves to remind us of the importance of considering the probability of the occurrence of Event 2 not just in the presence of Event 1, but also in its absence.

In sum, the previous examples neatly represent the three main scenarios for the relationship between two events, E1 and E2. First, these two events can maintain a generative/excitatory relationship, which is represented by a positive contingency ($\Delta P > 0$), as in the dog-compliance example. Second, the events can maintain a preventive/inhibitory relationship, which is represented by a negative contingency ($\Delta P < 0$), as in the TV-homework example. And third, the events might be unrelated, a case that is represented by a zero (or near zero) contingency ($\Delta P = 0$), as in the allergy medicine-insomnia example.

CONTINGENCY LEARNING EXPERIMENTS

The reader might have already realized the huge potential of this simple statistic, ΔP, in psychological research. Not surprisingly, there is a vast amount of research exclusively devoted to studying contingency judgments (the numerical estimation of the contingency between two events experienced by participants), most of it conducted with humans in the tradition now generally known as *human contingency learning*. This research became tremendously popular in the 1990s, when many research teams devoted their time to understanding whether actual contingency judgments do match the objective value of the contingency, that is, the ΔP statistic. The body of research on this matter is truly impressive[22] and a general agreement now exists that human contingency learning seems to fit well with the predictions of ΔP[23].

This is not to say that there was consensus among researchers on the mechanisms of learning. Saying that contingency judgments quite often concur with the objective contingency as measured by ΔP does not mean that one calculates ΔP in one's head in order to rate contingencies... or does it? In the 1990s, one of the fiercest battles was fought between those who defended the *statistical accounts* of contingency learning and those who defended the *associative accounts*, inherited from the animal conditioning tradition. Now the battle has seemingly subsided, but it has actually become more interesting, for a third party has joined it: the *inferential account*, which defends the role of higher-order cognitive processes (such as logical

---

[22] For representative publications, see Shanks, Medin, and Holyoak's (1996) special volume of *The psychology of learning and motivation* on causal learning. Some chapters in this book are particularly informative (see Baker, Murphy, & Vallée-Tourangeau, 1996; Shanks, Lopez, Darby, & Dickinson, 1996; Wasserman, Kao, Van Hamme, Katagiri, & Young, 1996), since they offer a plethora of graphs depicting the contingency ratings arising from different values of ΔP.

[23] Some interesting deviations from ΔP were found too, and they were the target of studies aiming to discriminate between statistical and associative accounts of learning.

inferences, hence its name) in the estimation of contingencies. The inferential account might be a theoretical framework on its own, but it seems to make better friends with the statistical approach than with the die-hard associative approach. It is not my goal to tell the story of this battle here[24], but rather, to just point out the obvious, that the general agreement on how well ΔP *describes* the results was just the seed for a fundamental disagreement on whether it can *explain* them.

RAT-ING CONTINGENCIES

It is not always explicitly recognized, but the original research on contingency learning was not carried out with humans. True, the field of human contingency learning is still a young, vibrant area of research[25], but it is not original; rather, it is just the offspring of earlier research performed with animals and, you guessed right, specifically with rats. And here it is where the patient reader will understand the reason for this rather long digression on contingency and ΔP: when it comes to the historic roots of the study of contingency learning, the rat was the first statistician[26]. In his influential work[27], Robert Rescorla overtly challenged contemporary belief in the necessity and sufficiency of contiguity (CS-US pairings) for the formation of conditioned responses, arguably setting the beginning of a new era in the study of classical (and instrumental) conditioning, by proposing a less than automatic, not so stimulus-response mediated, more cognition-spiced learning. This is clear even from the very title of his paper, which comprises

---

[24] For those interested in this topic, see De Houwer and Beckers (2002), Pineño and Miller (2007), and Shanks (2007).

[25] See Shanks (2007) for a recent historical review.

[26] Closely followed by the pigeon (see Wasserman, Franklin, & Hearst, 1974).

[27] Rescorla (1968).

a brief description of the ΔP statistic: *Probability of shock in the presence and absence of CS in fear conditioning.*

What did Rescorla do exactly in that paper? Nothing special, actually. He just manipulated the CS-US contingencies in a few groups of animals and then assessed their level of fear as indicated by the suppression ratio[28]. Of course, this is easy to say today, more than forty years after the publication of this paper. Framed in its historical context, however, this study was quite unorthodox, if not simply revolutionary. But, in order to fully appreciate the importance of this study, I first need to explain it in some detail.

In his first experiment, a group (Group G, for *gated*) was consistently given CS-US (tone-footshock) pairings. Conditioned fear elicited by the tone CS in this group was compared with that of two groups (Groups R-1 and R-2) given *random* presentations of the CS and the US. Specifically, in Group R-1, CS-US presentations were intermixed with additional US-alone presentations (exactly the same number as CS-US presentations). Thus, in Group R-1, the US presentations were programmed to occur with the same frequency both in the presence and in the absence of the CS or, in other words, independently from the CS presentations[29]. Group R-2

---

[28] The suppression ratio (Annau & Kamin, 1961) is related to the conditioned suppression of an ongoing instrumental response caused by the presentation of a fear-eliciting CS. The stronger the fear the CS elicits, the stronger the suppression of the appetitively-motivated instrumental response (for example, pressing a lever for food). The suppression ratio is calculated with a simple equation: $SR = A/A+B$, where A represents the number of responses during the CS presentation and B represents the number of responses prior to the CS presentation. Complete conditioned suppression is indicated by a SR value of 0.00, which is taken as indicative of strong fear. A SR value of 0.50 represents no conditioned suppression and, hence, no fear.

[29] Not to be mistaken with the treatment consisting of *explicitly unpaired* presentations. In that treatment, the CS and US presentations are programmed in such a way that the CS and the US cannot possibly coincide on a single trial. This difference is important: Rescorla's (1968) *random* treatment set a zero contingency between the CS and the US (they were completely independent from each other), whereas an explicitly unpaired treatment would effectively establish a *negative* contingency (the CS is learned to signal the absence of the US because, in this treatment, when the CS happens, the US does not happen, and *vice versa*).

aimed to control for a potential confound of Group R-1: because the treatment received by Group R-1 consisted of the same number of CS-US pairings received by Group G plus an identical number of US-alone presentations, this means that Group R-1 got twice as many US-presentations as Group G. Group R-2, just as Group R-1, received an equal share of CS-US and US-alone trials, with the total number of US presentations being identical to that of Group G.

The results of this experiment are clear-cut. Over the ten test sessions consisting of CS-alone presentations, Groups R-1 and R-2 showed no indication of conditioned fear (that is, their suppression ratios oscillated around 0.50), while Group G initially showed conditioned fear, which then extinguished throughout testing (that is, an initial suppression ratio of 0.00, which then increased to a value close to 0.50). This experiment thus proved that there is more to classical conditioning than just contiguity or CS-US pairings. Because Groups G and R-1 received exactly the same number of CS-US trials, their different levels of conditioned fear can only be due to the extra US-alone presentations received by Group R-1. The addition of US-alone trials degraded the CS-US contingency and, with it, the conditioning of fear to the CS. In other words, Rescorla found that the CS-US contingency seemed to strongly determine the animals' conditioned response, in spite of an identical number of CS-US pairings.

Do these results mean that rats can accurately perceive the CS-US contingency or that they can merely discriminate between contingent and non-contingent relationships? In other words, how sensitive are rats to different contingencies? Rescorla answered this question with a second experiment. In this experiment, the probabilities of the US in the presence and in the absence of the CS were independently manipulated in eight groups: .4-.4, .2-.2, .1-.1, 0-0, .4-.2, .4-.1, .4-0, .2-.1, .2-0, and .1-0. That is, despite the different frequencies in the US presentation, Groups .4-.4, .2-.2, .1-.1, 0-0 were exposed to an identical (zero) contingency. Not surprisingly, these four groups showed no sign of conditioned fear. More interesting, this experiment showed that, when the probability of the US in the presence of the CS (first number in the group names) was held constant, lowering the probability of the US in the absence of the CS (second number in the group names) resulted in a gradual increase in conditioned fear. Specifically, the following patterns were observed in conditioned fear, as indicated by the suppression ratios: .4-.4 < .4-.2 < .4-.1 < .4-0, and .2-.2 < .2-.1 < .2-0, and finally .1-.1 < .1-0. Therefore, these results support the conclusion from the previous experiment, namely, that conditioned fear was determined by the CS-US contingency, instead of merely the contiguity or number of CS-US pairings. Moreover, these results indicate that, far from merely discriminating between contingent and non-contingent relationships, rats are very sharp in telling apart varying degrees of CS-US contingencies.

The reader might now be wondering what this issue with contingencies is all about. Even if one understands what these experiments mean regarding a shift of focus from contiguity to contingency, it might still be difficult to see why this was so relevant; why these studies transformed our understanding of classical and instrumental conditioning at once, inviting us to leave behind the traditional view of conditioned reflexes and automatic stimulus-elicited responses, thereby allowing learning and behavior research to catch the train of cognitive psychology. Simply put, contingency-based responding means *informativeness*-mediated responding. This means that, depending on the specific CS-US[30] contingency, the CS will be processed as more or less informative about the occurrence (or nonoccurrence) of the US, thereby producing stronger or weaker responding.

To better explain this point, let us consider again Rescorla's second experiment, in which conditioned fear was found to be a

---

[30] Or R-O, as this applies to instrumental conditioning as well.

function of the CS-US contingency. When the contingency was 1 (for example, Groups .4-0, .2-0, and .1-0), the US only occurred in the presence of the CS. In this case, the CS provided very reliable information about the occurrence of the US (that is, the CS signaled the US) and, as a consequence, it elicited a strong fear response. By contrast, when the contingency was 0 (for example, Groups .4-.4, .2-.2, .1-.1, and 0-0), the US was equiprobable regardless of whether the CS was present or absent. In this case, the CS did not provide reliable information about the occurrence of the US (that is, the CS did not signal the US) and, accordingly, it did not elicit a fear response. Moreover, with intermediate contingencies (for example, Groups .4-.2, .4-.1, .2-.1), the CS adopted intermediate degrees of informative value, eliciting proportionally strong fear responses.

At the beginning of this section, I stated that contiguity "helps you narrow the list of things you might want to consider putting together in your mind". This list, however, is not always short enough. The coincidence in time and space (contiguity) of some events usually reflects their factual connection. Many times though, these coincidences are purely accidental. Our contingency detection system allows us to discard spurious coincidences, and to focus on relevant information provided by the regularities in our environment[31].

RAT, OPEN MINDED

In the present chapter I have discussed two topics that I consider representative of the change of view undergone during the last few decades by animal conditioning research, from a purely

---

[31] Consider again the examples previously used in this section to illustrate the calculation of ΔP. In the last example (allergy medicine and insomnia), we saw how a null contingency (a ΔP value close to zero) could be in place in spite of the frequent co-occurrence of two events. That is, in this example there was strong contiguity, but very poor contingency.

behavioral (that is, automatic, stimulus-response, mindless) to a more cognitive (that is, elaborated, processed, thought-mediated, mindful) framework. This constitutes a true paradigm shift, even a paradigm revolution[32]. Taken together, these two topics offer a brand new account of conditioning processes in animals. Far from merely reacting to stimuli due to prior contiguous CS-US pairings, the response elicited by the CS is a function of *what* this CS signals and *how reliably* it does so. In this view, the presentation of the CS activates a mental representation of the US. Furthermore, the nature of the US which memory is retrieved is responsible for the form (quality) of the conditioned response that the CS elicits, whereas the CS-US contingency or CS-informativeness determines the strength (quantity) of this conditioned response[33]. Similarly, instrumental or operant conditioning can be viewed as based on the combined effect of R-O contingency and the nature of the outcome. An instrumental response will be more or less likely to be made as a function of how effective it is in producing/removing an appetitive/aversive outcome – an outcome that, based in available experimental evidence, seems to be represented in the animal's mind and provides the motivation for the instrumental response to be made.

---

[32] Kuhn (1962).

[33] This could be viewed in two alternative ways. On one hand, it could be that the contingency value directly determines the strength in the activation of the US representation. On the other hand, it could be that the US representation is fully activated by the CS, with the contingency value then determining the expectation of the occurrence of the US and, hence, the strength of the conditioned response.

CHAPTER 4: MIND THE RAT

If the previous chapter had the expected effect on the reader, at this point we might agree that there is more to classical and operant conditioning than the simple S-R portrayal of behaviorism. But, if we are to make the case for our thinking rat, we will need more compelling evidence. In the present chapter, I review a selection of representative studies that, although technically conducted within the classical and operant paradigms, show evidence of higher-order cognitive processes in the rat.

LOGICALLY BLOCKED

Enter the blocking effect[1], the phenomenon that has historically been attributed the responsibility for the cognitive revolution of animal learning research[2]. Few phenomena in animal learning and human associative learning have been effectively explained from so many different theoretical viewpoints, from the traditional associative perspective to the statistical framework and, more recently, the inferential reasoning account. I will first briefly explain the blocking effect and then discuss recent findings regarding this phenomenon that will start, if not shattering, at least chipping away at old conceptions.

---

[1] Kamin (1968, 1969).

[2] The reason why Kamin's blocking effect has been historically awarded this merit is not directly due to its inherent interest, but due to its having inspired the most influential model of classical conditioning, the model of Rescorla and Wagner (1972), which in turn revolutionized the whole area. A cascade of new models of learning and hundreds of experiments were inspired, directly or indirectly, by this model.

BLOCKING BUSTERS

In a typical blocking experiment, animals are given two separate phases of treatment. The critical experimental condition (Blocking) receives, in the first phase, pairings of a CS, A,[3] with the US. In the second phase, this group receives further pairings of CS A with the US, but this time with a little twist: a second CS, X, is added during the presentation of CS A, thereby creating an AX compound stimulus. This second CS, X, is actually the target CS, and it is the CS that is later presented alone at test in order to assess its potential to evoke conditioned responding. With this treatment, the typical result consists of weak conditioned responding being elicited by CS X. Of course, "weak" is quite vague, and there is no absolute means to tell apart weak or strong responses. How weak this response is can only be determined by comparing it to the response elicited by CS X in a control condition. Among the many control conditions commonly employed, the one that has been generally regarded as the best choice (meaning, less open to alternative explanations), consists of replacing CS A with another CS, B, during the first phase of training. Thus, this control condition first receives pairings of CS B with the US, and then pairings of the AX compound with the US. When CS X is then presented at test in the control condition, strong responding is observed relative to that of the Blocking condition. The treatments of the Blocking and Control groups are summarized in the

---

[3] This nomenclature is typically used in the literature. In it, different letters represent different CSs (for example, CS A could be a tone, CS B could be another tone, CS C could be a light…). This nomenclature has the advantage of allowing us to simplify explanations of experimental designs/treatments, while detaching it from the specific CSs used in the explanation. In this system, the specific nature of each CS is not relevant. It does not matter whether CSs A and B are, say, a tone and a light, or sucrose and salt solutions, or different fictitious medicines on a computer screen (typical stimuli used in human contingency learning experiments). What matters is that CS A and B, are two different stimuli.

following table.

Group	Phase 1	Phase 2	Test	Result
Blocking	A-US	AX-US	X	Weak CR
Control	B-US	AX-US	X	Strong CR

Simplified design of a blocking experiment. A, B, and X are different CSs; AX means that CSs A and X are presented simultaneously.

In sum, in this experimental design, we have two groups, Blocking and Control, that receive identical treatment during Phase 2, consisting of compound presentations of CSs A and X, followed by the US (for example, presentations of a tone and a light, followed by footshock). For the Blocking group, CS A (the tone) was paired with the US on its own during Phase 1, whereas for the Control group, an alternative CS, B (for example, a noise), was paired with the US during Phase 1. At test, CS X (the light) is presented to both groups, resulting in weaker responding for the Blocking group than for the Control group.

Now, let us bring back some stuff from the previous chapter. In that chapter, I discussed the meaning and relevance of contingency learning to our understanding of conditioning phenomena and stated that, in the calculation of the CS-US (or R-O) contingency, the animal needs to contrast the probability of the US in the presence and in the absence of the CS. Therefore, strong conditioned responding to the CS is observed when US occurs more often in the presence of the CS than in its absence. Also, when the US happens equally often in the presence and absence of the CS, this CS elicits poor conditioned responding. Bearing this idea of contingency in mind, let us take another look at the previous table and pay attention to the treatments received by the Blocking and Control groups. The problem should now be obvious. Both groups are given an identical number of presentations of CS X with the US during Phase 2, and both groups are given an identical number of presentations of the US in the absence of CS X during

Phase 1. That is, the contingencies between the target CS, X, and the US are identical in both groups.

So, why does this CS elicit different responses (or, more correctly, the same response with different strengths) in each group? The only difference between the treatments received by the Blocking and Control groups, namely whether the CS-US pairings of Phase 1 involved the same CS presented in compound with CS X during Phase 2 (Blocking group) or a different CS (Control group), seems to be important enough for the animals in these experiments to "decide" whether to respond or not to CS X at testing.

And would it not be important for us too? Consider the following scenario. In order to lose some weight, you decide to take a medicine (call it Medicine A) that, although effective, makes you feel nauseated. Later, while still using this medication, you also take an over-the-counter drug (call it Medicine X) to deal with migraine (you are effectively taking two medicines, A and X, concurrently), still suffering nausea. Would you say that Medicine X is responsible for your illness? It might be tempting to conclude that Medicine X cannot be found responsible for the sickness, given that this symptom was already known to be produced by Medicine A alone. But, can you be sure of this? What if you took Medicine X alone and, still, you felt miserable? The truth is, you should remain skeptical about Medicine X. It could cause nausea, or it could not, you just cannot tell. Let us now assume that the fate of your drug prescription went slightly differently, and that you first had to take Medicine B to deal with arthritis, which causes (you guessed right) nausea. Then, once you stop taking Medicine B, you start your treatment with Medicine A (to lose weight), which you take along with Medicine X (for your migraines). As in the previous example, the cocktail of Medicines A and X results in nausea. In these circumstances, how certain would you be that Medicine X causes nausea? Although you have only experienced Medicine X along with Medicine A (and, thus, you cannot be fully certain of the role of Medicine X in causing nausea), in this case you did not have a prior history with Medicine A and nausea. Thus, both Medicines, A and X, could be equally responsible for your discomfort... which means that you might be a little more confident that Medicine X is to be blamed[4].

DECIDING TO FREAK OUT

The previous explanation of the blocking effect might have given the impression that such effect is the product of an elaborated reasoning process, something more similar to the job of an intuitive scientist. Although useful for illustrative purposes, one should be cautious with such an elaborate account. Indeed, the blocking effect can be perfectly explained by any associative model of learning based on simple processes resulting in the target CS, X, being impaired (or *blocked*) by the presence of CS A in its acquisition of an association with the US. That is, there is no need to appeal to any rational, logical decision process in order to explain this effect. Or is there?

Nobody would question that higher-order cognitive processes can play a critical role in human behavior. The ubiquity of *top-down processing* is commonplace in cognitive psychology, in which even "low-order" psychological processes such as perception, attention, learning, and memory can be affected by "higher-order" processes. Perhaps due to this reason, when experiments on the blocking effect that supported an inferential reasoning approach were performed with humans[5], the general reaction from the scientific

---

[4] Even in the control condition one could expect Medicine A to interfere with learning about the causal role of Medicine X. The compound training of two stimuli (CSs A and X) with the US is known to result in weaker responding to CS X relative to the elemental training of CS X with the US, an effect known as overshadowing (Pavlov, 1927).

[5] See, for example, Beckers, De Houwer, Pineño, and Miller (2005); De Houwer, Beckers, and Glautier (2002); Livesey and Boakes (2004); Lovibond, Been, Mitchell, Bouton, and

(Footnote continued on next page)

community, even from those who still preferred to stick to the old associative explanation, was the simple recognition of a long-suspected fact. These experiments brought very interesting new findings to the field, but admittedly made no waves. People were ready to embrace these results – at least for human research. What really shocked some of us was the series of experiments that demonstrated that some of these inferential processes also played a big role in the occurrence of the blocking effect in the rat.

The study in question was conducted by Tom Beckers and his collaborators[6] in a conditioned fear preparation, in which different CSs (different kinds of auditory stimuli and a light) were paired with a footshock US. In each of the three experiments in this study, half of the animals received a blocking treatment (A-US pairings followed by AX-US pairings) and the other half of the animals were given a control treatment (B-US pairings followed by AX-US pairings[7]). The critical treatment was given before the blocking or control treatment, during a pretraining phase. In this phase, the animals were provided with certain information that would presumably determine their subsequent reasoning about the interaction between the blocking and blocked CSs (A and X) with the US. In turn, this knowledge should then impact the occurrence and strength of the detected blocking effect. Specifically, the information provided during the pretraining phase regarded the *additivity* and *maximality* of the outcome (in these experiments, the footshock US). But, before I can elaborate on the study by Beckers and his collaborators, these two terms require some explanation.

The *outcome additivity* effect refers to the notion that the concurrent presentation of two (or more) causes of the same

---

Frohardt (2003); Mitchell and Lovibond (2002).

[6] Beckers, Miller, De Houwer, and Urushihara (2006).

[7] See previous section for a detailed explanation of the blocking effect.

outcome should have additive effects on the outcome intensity. That is, if each of two Causes, C and D, separately produce the outcome with a 50% intensity, the concurrent presentation of Causes C and D should produce the outcome with a 100% intensity. Think, for example, of the dangerous effect of combining the intake of a pill that causes drowsiness and alcohol on your driving skills. Independently, the pill or a couple of glasses of wine might impair your performance at the wheel, but perhaps not enough for you to get in an accident. But if you take the pill and drink some wine[8], the additive effects of being both drowsy and tipsy might be enough to send you off the road.

The inferential reasoning account relies on the outcome additivity assumption to explain the blocking effect. Basically, according to this viewpoint, during the pairings of Cause A with the outcome, Cause A is learned as a cause of the outcome. In fact, at this point, Cause A is *the* cause of the outcome, for its presence alone suffices to produce the outcome. Then, the compound presentation of Causes A and X is paired with the same outcome. Bearing outcome additivity in mind, what can we deduce from this treatment regarding the causal status of Cause X? Based on the assumption that combined causes of the same outcome should have an additive effect on the intensity of the outcome, one would expect that if X was also a valid cause of the outcome, the compound presentation of A and X should result in an even stronger outcome. But this is not the case. The outcome following the AX compound is identical to the outcome that previously occurred following Cause A alone. Once this is realized, the conclusion is clear: X does not alter the intensity of the outcome and, hence, it cannot be said to cause it. Thus, to answer our

---

[8] In real life, the combination of different causes might result in intricate interactions, but we still apply (quite wrongly) this simple assumption regarding the additivity of the outcomes of combined causes.

question, this line of reasoning ends with a low causal status of Cause X. This, in other words, is the blocking effect.

The *outcome maximality* effect is related to the outcome additivity effect. Specifically, it refers to the notion that one needs to experience a submaximal outcome (an outcome of less than maximal intensity) in order to be able to assess the outcome additivity effect. In other words, if we are to determine whether the concurrent presentation of two causes results in a more intense outcome than that produced by each of the causes separately, we need to be certain that the outcome experienced after the elemental presentation of each cause was of submaximal intensity. Consider what would happen if you first learned that Cause A produces a 100% intense outcome (an outcome of maximal intensity), and then you observed that the compound of Causes A and X also produces a 100% intense outcome. Could you determine that Cause X lacks causal value? In truth, you could not. In this scenario, it is possible for Cause X to produce the outcome as well, but because a complete or maximal outcome was already being produced by A alone, you just cannot determine if X plays a causal role. In order to be able to establish the causal value of X in this circumstances, you should first experience Cause A producing a submaximal outcome, say, a 50% intense outcome. If, after learning that Cause A results in a 50% intense outcome, you still observe the same 50% intense outcome following the AX compound, then it is safe to assume that X is not adding anything to the occurrence of the outcome – that is, X is not a valid cause of the outcome. If X had any causal power over the outcome, one would expect its intensity to be higher than 50% after the presentation of the AX compound (between a 50% and a 100% intensity, there is plenty of room for X to demonstrate its effectiveness). Importantly, only because Cause A produces an outcome of submaximal intensity (50%), the causal role of Cause X can be ruled out.

In sum, the outcome maximality effect can be considered a necessary precondition in order for the outcome additivity effect to play its role in the blocking effect. From this perspective, the blocking effect will only occur when submaximal outcomes are experienced, thus allowing the subject to determine whether the concurrent presentation of two or more causes has additive effects on the outcome intensity.

A problem with this explanation of the blocking effect based on the notions of outcome additivity and maximality is that it is not precisely parsimonious. Compared to the low-level processes proposed by associative models, this inferential account requires a certain set of elaborate assumptions to be implemented as a "standard program" in the individual's "mental software"[9]. As previously mentioned, this might be acceptable to many in regards to humans, but it will raise some eyebrows when it comes to rats. Thus, if we are to give some credit to the explanation of the blocking effect based on the outcome additivity and maximality effects, strong proof is needed.

What Beckers and his colleagues found in their experiments with rats is arguably excellent proof[10]. Their first two experiments directly assessed the outcome additivity assumption. In the first experiment, rats were given a treatment known to yield a strong blocking effect (or a control treatment thereof), preceded by either a pretraining session aiming to counteract the assumption of outcome additivity (a *subadditive* treatment), or an irrelevant control pretraining session. More precisely, the subadditive pretraining consisted of elemental presentations of CSs C and D with the US,

---

[9] Basically, this view implies that the regular blocking effect (with no additional explicit training) occurs because the individual assumes that: (1) The joint presentation of CSs A and X should yield a stronger US than following the presentation of A alone (outcome additivity) and, (2) that the US being experienced is not considered to be the strongest version of it (outcome maximality). How these assumptions could become part of a species standard (innate) mental program is yet to be explained by supporters of the inferential view.

[10] But see Haselgrove (2010) for an alternative account from an associative viewpoint.

interspersed with presentations of the CD compound CS, also paired with the US, with the intensity of the US being held constant on all trials. That is, the intensity of the US was identical following the presentation of C, D, and CD. Thus, the pretraining received by these rats disconfirmed the *a priori* assumption that the outcomes of compound causes have additive effects (because CD produced the same US intensity as C and D elementally). The question was whether this pretraining would affect the observation of the blocking effect for these rats, relative to the rats given an irrelevant (but related) pretraining[11]. And it did, the blocking effect was observed in the two conditions given an irrelevant pretraining, but not in the condition given the subadditive pretraining.

The second experiment by Beckers and his colleagues tried to obtain the mirror image of the results of the first experiment. That is, instead of using the additivity pretraining to impair an otherwise effective blocking treatment, this pretraining was used to enhance an otherwise ineffective blocking treatment. Therefore, in the second experiment, a treatment known to produce poor blocking was given to the rats. This poor blocking treatment was preceded by a pretraining aiming to restate or highlight the additivity property of the outcome, or by an irrelevant (control) pretraining. The additive pretraining consisted of elemental presentations of CSs C and D, paired with a US of the same intensity as that used in the previous experiment (a 0.7-mA footshock), interspersed with presentations of the CD compound, paired with a more intense US (a 1.0-mA footshock). Such additive pretraining was expected to enhance the strength of the blocking effect by reinforcing the "expectation" that, if the target CS, X, had any causal value, its

---

11 It is important to highlight here that the blocking treatment was carried out with CSs different from those used in the pretraining phase. The idea was to assess whether the information learned during the pretraining experience with CSs C and D (and the CD compound) would then affect the processing of CSs A and X during the blocking treatment.

causal role should become evident during the presentations of the compound CS, AX. Because this expectation would be then disconfirmed, the blocking effect should take place. The results of this experiment were in agreement with the predictions, at least to an extent[12].

In sum, the first two experiments in the study of Beckers and his collaborators showed the important role played by the outcome additivity notion in the occurrence of the blocking effect. When the outcome additivity notion was counteracted by the pretraining experience (first experiment) poor blocking was found. Conversely, when the pretraining experience supported the notion of outcome additivity (second experiment), the blocking effect was enhanced.

The last experiment of Beckers and his colleagues examined the outcome maximality effect. In this experiment, the pretraining stage actually consisted of preexposure to the US with different intensities (the footshock could be of 0.4, 0.75, or 1.0 mA). The intensity of the US was also manipulated during the subsequent blocking (or control) treatment. Specifically, the US could be of either maximal or submaximal intensity. That is, the footshock employed during the blocking treatment could be either the strongest or the weakest of the footshocks previously experienced[13]. Remember that outcome maximality was expected to determine the

---

[12] The additive pretraining did enhance the observed blocking effect relative to one of the conditions given an irrelevant pretraining (as expected), but not relative to the other irrelevant condition, which also showed a strong blocking effect. This result does not necessarily constitute a failure. In fact, the authors provided some *post hoc* explanations for the observation of this unexpectedly strong blocking effect in that irrelevant condition.

[13] More specifically, the maximal condition was preexposed to the 0.4-mA and 0.75-mA footshocks, and then received 0.75-mA footshocks during the blocking treatment. For one of the submaximal conditions (as for the maximal condition), preexposure consisted of presentations of the 0.4-mA and 0.75-mA footshocks. However, this submaximal condition then received 0.4-mA footshocks during the blocking treatment. For the other submaximal condition (as for the maximal condition), 0.75-mA footshocks were given during the blocking treatment. However, for this submaximal condition preexposure consisted of presentations of the 0.75-mA and 1.0-mA footshocks.

occurrence of the blocking effect because of its relation to the outcome additivity effect. If, and only if, a submaximal US was employed during the blocking treatment, the animals would be able to ascertain whether the addition of X during the concurrent presentation of CSs A and X resulted in a stronger US (the assumption of outcome additivity) and, hence (after determining that X seemingly had no impact on the US intensity), result in the observation of the blocking effect. The results of this experiment were clear. As predicted, the blocking effect was missing in the maximal condition, but was detected in both submaximal conditions.

The reader might still remain unconvinced. As interesting as the findings of Beckers and collaborators are, they might just be an isolated case. But this study is not a rare gem in the scientific literature. In fact, it was coincidentally followed by the publication of a few independent studies also showing evidence of higher-order cognition in the rat. The rest of this chapter is devoted to these studies. So please keep reading... the story is just about to get even more interesting.

EVERYTHING HAPPENS FOR A REASON

Since the original demonstrations of instrumental learning by Thorndike, closely followed by the extensive research conducted by Skinner in operant conditioning, it was well established that animals can learn from the consequences of their behavior. This fact has always been uncontroversial among learning theorists; after all, a behavioral change can be directly observed and, hence, leaves no room for debate about its existence. Say that a rat (for our convenience, we will call it Rat #1) is given food contingent upon pressing a lever and, as a consequence, this rat progressively presses the lever more frequently. By contrast, another rat (Rat #2), which is given free food regardless of its lever pressing, shows no change in the rate of lever press behavior. In this situation, it is safe to say that the reinforcement of lever pressing for Rat #1 was due to the presentation of food contingent upon the lever press response. But, can we assume that, because Rat #1 learned to perform the lever press response more often, this rat understands that its behavior causes the delivery of food? This question first appeared, more or less implicitly, in the previous chapter, when I discussed evidence of outcome representations in operant conditioning[14]. Simply put, these studies show that rats produce an operant response in order to achieve a very specific outcome, and that they seem to have such outcome in mind while producing the operant response. As was stated in that chapter, this is compatible with the view of operant behavior as goal-directed action. However, even if we accept that the rat's operant response is somehow connected to a more or less detailed mental representation of the outcome, the question still applies: does this mean that the rat *understands* that the outcome is caused by its response?

REBEL WITHOUT A CAUSE

We, humans, find it hard to envision a world without causality. We are so good at causal understanding that we can hardly apprehend other, more simple, possibilities. We know that our actions produce certain consequences and, therefore, we act in a purposeful manner, with the conscious intention of producing the consequences that deterministically follow our actions. Furthermore, we can reflect on our actions and their consequences and accordingly elaborate plans of action, evaluating their possible consequences in our own mind (mental simulation[15]). Thinking in causal terms is so normal for us that, if anything, we tend to see

---

[14] Colwill and Rescorla (1986).

[15] For a recent interdisciplinary work on this topic, see Markman, Klein, and Suhr (2008).

causality not only when there is only covariation[16], but also when there is no covariation at all[17]. It is certainly difficult for us to grasp the notion of behavior without causal understanding, of action without intention.

Still, instrumental behavior does not necessarily require causal understanding. A rat might be able to perform an operant response to obtain food, without fully understanding that its action (and only its action) is making the food available. All the rat needs to learn is that its response covaries with food, regardless of whether or not causation underlies this covariation. In fact, this is the view of associative theories. According to these theories, the association between response and outcome is formed based on the covariation (contingency) between these two events, and incorporates no information regarding the causal nature of the relationship between the response and the outcome. If the associative viewpoint was right, this story would be congruent with recent evidence in nonhuman primates showing that they find it difficult to pass strict tests for understanding the physical causal mechanisms underlying their use of tools[18]. Considering that tool use has been traditionally viewed as one of the most compelling demonstrations of causal understanding, claiming that apes and some species of monkeys can use tools without understanding the underlying mechanisms seems congruent with the idea that the rat or, for that sake, any animal can operate on its environment through its behavior without

---

[16] Think of how often those correlations discovered by epidemiologists are quickly converted by the media and, unluckily, by many scientists (who should know better) into causal relations. For example, the discovery that certain vaccines presumably correlated with the incidence of autism in the population soon became the rapidly spreading news about vaccines that cause autism. Now this idea prevails in spite of recent evidence disproving it (see http://tinyurl.com/yku8z48) and even when the original study making such claim has been retracted, twelve years later, by the journal that originally published it (see http://tinyurl.com/yg77b69 for the retraction notice).

[17] I provide a detailed discussion of the topic of *superstitious behavior* in Chapter 6.

[18] For a recent review, see Penn and Povinelli (2007).

understanding its causal role[19].

TO CAUSE OR NOT TO CAUSE, THAT IS THE QUESTION

Rats do not use tools, let alone understand the physical mechanisms underlying the way they work. So, should we just discard the possibility of causal understanding in the rat and move on? Fortunately not, for a handful of researchers decided that this question was important enough to deserve being tested. A fascinating line of research conducted by Aaron Blaisdell and his collaborators[20] has recently demonstrated the rat's ability to understand causal relations, as well as to tell apart the effects of its own actions from the effects of external events. As in the study of Beckers and collaborators (see previous section), the research of Blaisdell and collaborators consisted of a straightforward application to animal conditioning of ideas originally tested in humans[21]. The ideas in question are quite complex, and involve the predictions of different theories of learning (associative, statistical, and the more recently developed causal Bayes nets). However, these

---

[19] The observation that nonhuman primates can use tools while seemingly failing to understand the causal mechanisms underlying their use might well be one of those traits that set us, humans, apart from other animals. This might be true in regards to simple tools (say, a hammer or screwdriver), but what about the more complex tools we frequently use? How many of us can drive a car, or use a cell phone or a computer, without understanding how these things work? While using a tool does not require understanding, making a tool or, for the sake, repairing it does. By these standards, many of us (me included) fail to meet Penn and Povinelli's (2007) criteria.

[20] See Blaisdell, Sawa, Leising, and Waldmann (2006). Also see Leising, Wong, Waldmann, and Blaisdell (2008).

[21] For the original research that inspired the study of Blaisdell and cols. (2006), see Waldmann and Hagmayer (2005; also see Sloman and Lagnado, 2005). Ironically, while the original study in humans by Waldmann and Hagmayer received attention exclusively in the scientific community, its rat *alter ego* had a much broader impact, even appearing in the news. Alas, this kind of public interest might reflect, at least in part, the little credit we normally give to the rat (or, for the sake, any other "lowly" animal). For the media, a causal reasoning study in humans is tantamount to "dog bites man", whereas a study showing causal reasoning in the rat is tantamount to "man bites dog".

ideas are so fundamental, so "common sense" to us, that their explanation does not require of understanding of the theories. In fact, this is one of those cases in science in which a good example can perfectly do the job of lengthy explanations[22]. Consider the following scenario. A mailbox with a flag up indicates that the owner of the mailbox left something in it for collection. Thus, the postman will accordingly open the mailbox for collection only when the flag is up. This time, however, while delivering the mail the postman accidentally put the flag up. Should he, therefore, now open the mailbox in order to collect the mail? Obviously, the answer is no. We know that the flag being up normally signals that the mailbox contains mail for collection, but the flag does not cause the mailbox to contain mail. The mail in the mailbox and the flag being up are covarying events that certainly hold no causal relation. Rather, they are both effects of a common cause, the actions of the owner of the mailbox.

In order to recreate this scenario in their study with rats, Blaisdell and his collaborators gave their animals an experimental treatment consisting of the separate presentation of two types of trials, light-tone pairings and light-food pairings. The light was expected to be learned as a *common cause* of both the tone and the food (similar to the previous example, in which the owner of the mailbox was a common cause for the flag being up and the mail). These two trial types were given separately to prevent the animals from learning a direct association between the tone and the food. The following figure depicts this scenario.

---

[22] See Clayton and Dickinson (2006) for a good example involving hung laundry, rain, and a sprinkler. Also see Leising and cols. (2008) for another great example, this one involving the weather, atmospheric pressure, and barometer readings.

Graphical representation of the common-cause model. After receiving presentations of the light followed separately by the tone and by food, the rat presumably learns the light as a common cause of the tone and the food.

The question now is whether the rat can understand that the light is a common cause for the tone and the food. If so, upon hearing the tone, the rat should infer that it was caused by the light, which also implies that food should be available. (Note that, when the tone is presented alone, the light was not presented. However, like us, rats might deduce that the fact that the light was not seen does not necessarily mean that it never occurred – they might have just missed it.) If the rat follows this rationale, upon hearing the tone, it should go to the food hopper to check for food, thereby producing a nose poke (the dependent variable in this study). But, again, observing this result does not guarantee the rat's understanding of the light-tone and light-food relationships as causal. Exactly the same result could be expected if the rat had merely learned that the light covaries with both the tone and the food, without necessarily causing their occurrence. Regardless of the causal nature of the light-tone and light-food relations, what matters is that the tone always goes with the light, and the light always goes with the food. Hence, the tone means that food has been served.

In order to ascertain if rats truly understand the causal structure underlying the relationships involving the light, the tone, and the food, Blaisdell and his collaborators then introduced an ingenious manipulation in their experimental treatment. They allowed some of the animals in their experiment to directly cause the occurrence of the tone by making an operant response (lever press). In other words, they allowed the rats to intervene in the occurrence of the tone (a situation comparable to that of the postman personally putting up the flag in our example). The study of Blaisdell and collaborators included two main conditions. Both conditions first received light-tone and light-food pairings, thereby giving the opportunity to learn a common-cause model (the light causes both the tone and the food). Afterwards, one of the conditions (Intervene) learned that they could control the occurrence of the tone by pressing the lever whereas, in the other condition (Observe), the tone was given independently of the lever press response. This, in other words, corresponds to the difference between learning about causal relations from "seeing" (observational learning) and "doing" (interventional learning).

The results of the study were clear. Upon hearing the tone, the rats in Condition Observe nose poked significantly more than the rats in Condition Intervene. Simply put, the animals seemingly understood that the tone was a reliable signal for food, but only when occurring on its own. Presumably, when the tone happened without intervention, its occurrence was attributed to the light, which in turn meant that food had been presented as well. By contrast, when the tone was the product of an intervention, the light was discounted as the cause of the tone, which also indicated the absence of food[23]. This is represented in the following figure.

---

[23] Further support to this conclusion comes from an additional condition in this experiment, referred to as the *direct-cause* condition, in which a noise was directly paired with food. In this condition, as in the *common-cause* condition, the noise could either appear on its own (Observe) or as a product of the rat's lever pressing (Intervene). However, contrary to the results of the common-cause condition, in the direct-cause condition a comparably high number of nose pokes were observed regardless of whether the noise appeared on its own or following a lever press. This finding makes sense in this condition because, in a direct-cause model, the noise indicates the presence of food regardless of

(Footnote continued on next page)

Graphical representation of the result of an intervention in the common-cause model. The rat's lever press behavior causes the occurrence of the tone. As a consequence, the animal infers that the tone was not caused by the light. Thus, no food is expected.

Therefore, the results of this study show that the rats not only understood the relationship between the light and the tone and food as causal, but they also understood the relationship between their own behavior and the tone as causal. That is, they understood that their behavior caused the tone's occurrence, which implies that they seem to be pretty aware of their role as causal agents. It is important to remark that these results necessarily imply that the animals correctly understood that the light was a common *cause* for both the tone and the food. If all they had previously learned was that the light simply covaried with the tone and the food (as predicted by associative theories of learning), upon experiencing the tone they should nose poke for food, regardless of whether the tone had occurred on its own or due to their intervention.

The study by Blaisdell and collaborators included additional conditions that helped these conclusions to be drawn and firmly established. In one such condition, rats received a treatment involving the light, the tone, and food, as well as the subsequent split between observation and intervention treatments. However, this condition received tone-light pairings, instead of light-tone

---

whatever caused its occurrence.

pairings (the presentation of the tone now preceded the presentation of the light). This procedural change, although seemingly small, dramatically changes the underlying causal structure of this treatment. This condition, given tone-light pairings interspersed with light-food pairings, promotes the learning of a causal chain like the one depicted in the following figure.

Graphical representation of the causal-chain model. After receiving separate presentations of the tone followed by the light, and of the light followed by food, the rat presumably learns the tone causes the light, which in turn causes the food.

Interestingly, contrary to the common-cause model, in a causal-chain model no difference is expected between the animals in a group given mere exposures to the tone (Condition Observe) and the animals that were given the chance to cause the tone (Condition Intervene). Regardless of whether the tone happened "spontaneously" (Observe) or "artificially" (Intervene), the presence of the tone means that the light should also occur, which in turn should result in the presentation of food. Accordingly, in both conditions the rats nose poked (checked for food) regularly after the occurrence of the tone[24]. This is represented in the

---

[24] Interestingly, the rats nose poked after the tone presentation even when the light was not presented on the test trials. Should the absence of the expected light not disrupt this causal chain, thereby diminishing the expectation of food? Not if the animals assumed that the light occurred, but was somehow missed – something possible since the light bulb had been previously removed by the experimenters. (See section *Keep it real* in Chapter 3 for a related study, actually inspired by this finding.)

following figure.

Graphical representation of an intervention in the causal chain model. The rat's lever press behavior causes the occurrence of the tone, which signals the presentation of the light and, therefore, of food.

It thus seems that rats can form veridical representations of the causal structure underlying their environment, and adapt their behavior accordingly[25]. It also seems that they can tell apart events caused by the environment from events caused by their own actions[26]. Thus, we can now consider the original question of this section affirmatively answered. Based on the available evidence, it is fair to state that the rat seems to understand that the outcome is caused by its own response. Rats behave in a purposeful manner, with the intention of producing a specific outcome. That is, operant conditioning *is* goal-directed action. In fact, a recent study[27] has shown that, for rats, actions have a prominent status as candidate

---

[25] A recent article by Dwyer, Starns, and Honey (2009) challenged the conclusions of Blaisdell and his collaborators. According to Dwyer and cols., the findings of Blaisdell and cols. (2006) can be explained as merely due to response competition, specifically due to the interference caused by lever pressing on nose poking (in Condition Intervene, but not in Condition Observe). If the claim of Dwyer and cols. is right (something that future research will certainly elucidate), the validity of the study of Blaisdell and cols. as evidence of causal reasoning in rats will be severely damaged. (This is not to say that this issue is already resolved: in a chapter still in preparation, Blaisdell and Waldmann provide additional analysis of their experimental data that, they claim, disconfirm the account of Dwyer et al. This promises to be a very fruitful and interesting scientific battle.)

[26] Also see Killeen (1978) for similar evidence with pigeons.

[27] Leising and cols. (2008).

causes for events occurring in the environment. This study used the common-cause model to compare the impact of an intervention (an instrumental response causing the occurrence of a tone) with that of an exogenous cue (an external stimulus causing the occurrence of a tone). When the tone followed an action (intervention), as in the study of Blaisdell and collaborators, the rats did not nose poke to check for food (again, presumably because the intervention resulted in discounting the role of the light as the cause of the occurrence of the tone and, thus, the likelihood that food had also been presented). By contrast, when the tone followed the exogenous cue, the rats still nose poked for food, a result that indicates that the exogenous cue failed to discount the role of the light as the cause of the occurrence of the tone.

A NOTE ON PREDICTION AND CAUSALITY

The aforementioned results[28] seem to be congruent with the common notion that instrumental action is causal in nature, whereas relations among environmental stimuli can be either predictive or causal[29]. This bias is not exclusive to the rat. We, humans, also perceive our actions as strongly causally linked to their consequences. I am now typing on my computer and my behavior (pressing keys on my laptop) is followed by specific consequences (letters and punctuation signs appearing on the computer screen). Perceiving the relationship between my behavior and its outcome as merely covariational is not enough – this is causality in action. The same cannot be said, however, about environmental events. Here covariation might lead to causation, but only under certain

---

[28] Ibid.

[29] Of course, the exogenous cue could have perfectly been a cause of the tone. However, processing of an external stimulus as causal seems to require of extensive experience with the stimulus, whereas intentional actions (operant behaviors) seem to be processed as causal by default (see meta-analysis in Leising and cols., 2008).

conditions (for example, enough exposure to the covarying events to draw conclusions, sufficient contingency in their occurrence, etc.). This difference between actions and external events regarding their *a priori* causal status might just reflect a straightforward psychological adaptation to the real causal texture of our world. Out there, in our environment, there are merely covarying events and true causal relations. Determining which of these events maintain a purely covariational relationship and which ones are causally related is of critical importance. Although learning about both covariation and causation is extremely useful in order to *predict* the occurrence of certain events, learning about causation also allows us to *manipulate* their occurrence.

Let us first consider an instance of covariation in the absence of causation. Learning that a flashing red light at a railroad crossing predicts that a train is coming might be of great importance for your survival (you might want to keep distance from an approaching train). However, there is not much you can do to prevent the train from coming (turning the flashing red light off will not make the train go away). In this case, you learn that the light predicts, but does not cause the occurrence of the train[30], and thus you learn that you cannot control the occurrence of the event (the train will come, no matter what you do), but you can still adapt your behavior to the occurrence of such event (staying away from the railroad).

Now let us examine an instance of covariation involving causation. Imagine that, upon entering into someone's home, you always start sneezing uncontrollably. Because you do not want to offend this person, you keep visiting her every now and then, each time fearing another horrible time sneezing out loud. After some

---

[30] In fact, things are slightly more complicated: the light is a consequence of the approaching train. The flashing of the red light is programmed to happen in order to allow people like you to predict the imminence of the train.

medical tests, you discover that you are allergic to cats, and your friend happens to have two. Asking her to put the cats away in a separate room while you are visiting, as rude as it sounds, could save you some sneezes and will help you (and your friend) enjoy the visit. That is, causal learning allows us to, not only predict, but also control the occurrence of certain events by manipulating their causes. If knowledge is power, then causal knowledge is the ultimate power. Sometimes, however, we can learn what we consider to be a true causal relationship, yet manipulating the cause is not a possibility. For example, one can learn that black clouds usually precede a storm. Unfortunately, we cannot remove the black clouds (or change the weather conditions that produce them) in order to make the storm go away, but we can still make use of the predictive value of the cause in order to adapt our behavior (for example, we can look for shelter or just get an umbrella) to avoid a shower.

In the previous discussion, I mentioned the basic difference between predictive and causal learning and said that, while predictive learning allows us to adapt our behavior to an event, causal learning also allows us to manipulate the cause in order to produce or eliminate its effect. Now, if we think carefully about this, it will soon become apparent that I was making an important assumption, namely, that our manipulation, our own behavior, is in turn causally related with the cause we are manipulating. That is, after learning that one event causes another event (a cause-effect relation, or $C{\rightarrow}E$) we automatically, without much conscious thinking, manipulate the cause to either maximize or minimize the effect, something that can be translated into an action-cause-effect relation ($A{\rightarrow}C{\rightarrow}E$). This then takes us full circle back to the statement opening this section: we can learn causal relationships among external events, but the causal nature of our own actions seems to be implicitly assumed by default, almost without any need of explicit learning.

ARE CSS PREDICTORS OR CAUSES?

The research thus far discussed in this chapter suggests that, for the rat, stimulus-stimulus relations in Pavlovian conditioning are causal, instead of predictive, in nature. In the study of Beckers and collaborators, the notions of outcome additivity and maximality were found to play a role in the blocking effect, as found in conditioning involving CS-US pairings. In the study of Blaisdell and collaborators, the rats appreciably understood the light-tone and light-food relationships as forming a common-cause model, in which the light was the cause for both the tone and the food (as evidenced by the differential effects of merely observing the occurrence of the tone or intervening in its occurrence on the subsequent nose poking for food).

Causal processing of CS-US or CS-CS relations is at odds with a traditional understanding of Pavlovian conditioning as a paradigm of predictive learning[31]. In a classical conditioning experiment, the experimenter picks a stimulus (for example, a light or tone), which then serves as a CS that will signal the occurrence of another stimulus (for example, another CS or US). The CS does not cause the US (if anything, they are both caused by the Skinner box based on the sequence of events previously programmed by the experimenter). Like the flashing red light at a railroad crossing, the CS just predicts the US. And, yet, research findings indicate that the rat appears to disagree with our analysis – where there is covariation without causation, the rat seemingly sees a causal relation[32].

Previously in this chapter I discussed the possibility that the rat might not be able to understand the causal role played by its own actions in connection with the occurrence of the outcome. I am now stating that, not only does the rat seem to understand that

---

[31] Dickinson (1980).

[32] See Polack, McConnell, & Miller (2010) for further support to this conclusion.

its actions can cause outcomes, but the rat also seems to be sensitive to the causal structure of its environment. Furthermore, as I have just mentioned, the rat is seemingly biased towards causal processing of environmental events even in the absence of true causality. I previously stated that "thinking in causal terms is so normal for us that, if anything, we tend to see causality not only when there is only covariation, but also when there no covariation at all". Apparently, we are not the only causally biased animal.

THIS IS WHAT I KNOW...

Research like that previously discussed in this chapter, although conducted in the learning theory tradition, can easily fit into the category of animal cognition as well. That is, while these studies aim to merely understand learning processes in nonhuman animals, they provide us with great *insights* into the intelligence of these animals[33]. So, now we know that animals do think. Let us then just push our questions a little bit further and ask: can animals think about the contents of their own minds? In other words, do nonhuman animals have the property we call *metacognition* (meaning "cognition about cognition" or "thinking about thinking")? It is obvious that we, humans, have this quality. In fact, this topic has been one important source of philosophical arguments since the early times of Socrates ("One thing only I know, and that is that I know nothing") and, later, Descartes[34] (*cogito ergo sum*, "I think, therefore I am"). Philosophical as it sounds, the question of metacognition in nonhuman animals is purely psychological and,

---

[33] More than a century after the publication of Romanes' (1882) *Animal intelligence*, this term is still widely used to refer to the intelligence of nonhuman animals, perhaps because traditionally the study of the intelligence of animals (with an ethological and evolutionary orientation) had nothing to do with the study of human intelligence (with an psychometric orientation, that is, about testing IQ).

[34] Descartes (1637).

thus, open to experimental testing[35]. This is, in fact, what Foote and Crystal[36] did in their metacognition study with rats.

In order to better understand the experiment by Foote and Crystal, let us consider first an analogous human scenario. Imagine that you are taking a chemistry course in which, so far, you have not done too well. After taking the five mandatory quizzes, your grade in the course is disappointing – just a C. Your only chance to get a better grade is the final exam, which is optional. If you do not take it, you will have to stick to your grade of C. But if you took it and did well, you could raise your overall course grade up to a nice B. Now, here is the catch: if you take the exam and do poorly, your grade will sink down to a D. Because you can still leave your exam blank without penalty, you decide to give it a chance. After a long night of studying for the exam, you are now sitting at the desk and your professor leaves a copy of the exam in front of you. It will take you a few seconds to scan the questions and realize that you can do great on this exam – or that you are better off leaving the classroom right away. The parallel between this fictitious scenario (unfortunately for many students, not so fictitious) and Foote and Crystal's experiment will soon become evident, but the reader might appreciate already the relationship between this situation and the topic in discussion. In this situation, your answers to the questions depend on your knowledge of the lessons you were expected to study, whereas your very decision to take the exam will be based on your confidence on your own knowledge. That is, your decision is made based on whether you think you have the knowledge required

---

[35] The underlying logic is the same as for any other experiment in animal cognition: as any other cognitive process, metacognition itself must serve an adaptive purpose. In order to improve an individual's chances of survival, this psychological process needs to translate into adaptive behavior (knowing what you know and what you do not know, as interesting as it sounds, will not save your life if you do not behave accordingly). Thus, one should be able to study the behavioral correlates of metacognition in the animal laboratory.

[36] Foote and Crystal (2007).

for success. Simply put, you can blame a cognitive error for your wrong answers on the exam, but you should blame a metacognitive error for your having taken the exam in the first place[37].

Rats do not take exams. But rats, we have seen already, are good at "studying" stimulus relations in the Skinner box and "taking tests" responding on the different manipulanda (levers, nose poke apertures...) of such device. That is, the old Skinner box, a benchmark of radical behaviorism, once again offers a tool for the study of a *mental* process[38].

The ingenious experiment by Foote and Crystal recreated our "exam situation" in rats by giving the animals a stimulus duration discrimination test with stimulus presentations ("questions") of varying difficulty. Their working hypothesis was simple: if allowed, a rat might more likely decline responding as the "question" becomes more difficult. To answer this question, first they trained their rats to discriminate between "short" and "long" stimulus durations. The animals were given presentations of a stimulus (a noise) of varying duration, from 2 seconds to 8 seconds, and differentially reinforced for correctly identifying the noise as short (shorter than 4 seconds) or long (longer than 4 seconds)[39]. Specifically, after each stimulus presentation, the rats could press one of two levers (right lever vs. left lever) to earn a reward (food), with the reward being provided if, and only if, they pressed the

---

[37] The exam example, although good for illustrative purposes, does not represent the adaptive importance of metacognition. But imagine how the accuracy of your metacognition would become relevant if you were to eat, say, wild berries or mushrooms and you knew that, while generally safe and nutritious, some specimens could be poisonous and potentially lethal... and you relied on your ability to tell them apart.

[38] Ironic as this is, it also provides a perfect example of how it is possible for revolutionary research to be conducted within the established paradigm.

[39] The 4-second value (instead of 5 seconds) is the midpoint in a logarithmic scale (for example, the absolute differences between 2 and 4 and between 4 and 8 are identical in this scale). The reason underlying their use of a logarithmic scale is rooted in the Weber-Fechner law of psychophysics, as applied to perception of sounds.

correct lever, that is, the lever associated with the duration (short vs. long) of the stimulus just presented. Thus, if the stimulus being presented was short (from 2 to 4 seconds), the animals were rewarded for pressing the "short" lever, but not the "long" lever. Conversely, if the stimulus being presented was long (from 4 to 8 seconds), the animals were rewarded for pressing the "long" lever, but not the "short" lever. Now, as the reader can imagine, as simple as this task is, its difficulty lies in the actual duration of the stimulus being presented. While stimuli of the shortest and longest durations within the range (2 and 8 seconds) should be easily identified as short and long stimuli, respectively, the identification of stimuli close to the midpoint in duration (for example, 3.62 and 4.42 seconds) should be less clear. One would therefore expect more errors in discriminating stimuli with intermediate durations.

Foote and Crystal tested this prediction, but added a twist to the plot: the rats were sometimes allowed to decline to respond. On two-thirds of the test trials, two nose-poke apertures were illuminated. By nose poking on each of these apertures, the rats could either choose to take the test or decline to take the test. For example, poking on the right aperture would result in declining to take the test, whereas poking on the left aperture would result in taking the test. This voluntary test was referred to as a "choice test". On the other third of the test trials, only the nose-poke aperture corresponding to taking the test (the left aperture, following our example) was illuminated. That is, on these trials the rats were forced to take the test. The amount of reward given to the animals depended on whether they took the test or not and, if they did, on their performance in it. When the animals took the test, a correct response (correctly identifying the stimulus duration as short or long) provided 6 pellets of food, whereas an incorrect response provided 0 pellets. If the animals declined the test, 3 pellets were given automatically. Thus, the first choice for the animals in this situation is between a small, but guaranteed reward (3 pellets) if the test is declined or the possibility of a larger, but not guaranteed reward (6 pellets) if the test is taken.

The rationale of this experiment can now be fully appreciated. If, upon presentation of the stimulus, the rats were able to estimate their chances of correctly discriminating its duration or, in other words, if the rats *knew whether they knew the answer to the test*, they should be able to accordingly choose to take or decline the test. In sum, two predictions were made regarding the results of the experiment. The first prediction was that, when the animals were forced to take the discrimination test, they would make more errors with stimuli of intermediate durations (for example, 3.62 and 4.42 seconds) than with stimuli of very short or very long durations (that is, within the duration range of 2 and 8 seconds). The second prediction was that, when the animals were offered a choice between taking or declining the test, they would be more likely to decline the test as a function of the difficulty of the test, that is, when the stimulus being presented was of an intermediate duration. The results of the experiment supported both of these predictions. The rats seemingly knew their limits and, when given a choice to take the test, they decided to either take it or decline it as a function of the difficulty of the test. In fact, the rats declined to take precisely the choice tests with intermediate stimulus durations, that is, those durations that resulted in a high rate of errors in forced tests. This means that they declined to take the test when they did not know the answer. In turn, this indicates that they knew when they knew (and when they did not know) the answer to the test, something that evidences their metacognition[40].

We can now go back to the chemistry exam situation and fully see its parallel with Foote and Crystal's experiment. In this

---

[40] But see Staddon, Jozefowiez, and Cerutti (2007), for an alternative explanation. For further discussion, also visit the website of journal *Comparative Cognition & Behavior Reviews* (Volume 4 of 2009) for a special section devoted to metacognition: http://psyc.queensu.ca/ccbr.

experiment, when given the choice, the rats took the test (lever pressing) when they considered that the question (the stimulus duration) was easy enough to guarantee their getting a grade of B (6 pellets of food), and declined the test when the question was too difficult and likely to give them a D (0 pellets of food). In this latter case, instead of taking the risk, they chose to decline the test and stick to a grade of C (3 pellets of food). Certainly, rats do not go to college (at least, not to get a degree) and they do not take exams[41], but they can take tests – and they can estimate how well they will do depending on the test difficulty.

SIMPLE NO MORE

In this chapter I have discussed three separate lines of research that, although concerned with different cognitive processes (inferential reasoning, causal reasoning, and metacognition), converge in their delivery of a single take-home message: the mental processes underlying the behavior of the laboratory rat are much richer than we ever anticipated before. The rat, it seems, is especially prepared to deal with causal relations, be it among external events or between its own behavior and external events. Interestingly, the rat does not simply acquire and store information on the causal texture of its environment in a passive manner. Rather, it seems to actively process this information (inferential and causal reasoning), while keeping track of the limits of its own knowledge (metacognition). The result is a behavior more finely tuned to the demands of the environment. This animal no longer fits in the traditional view of an organism that automatically reacts to stimuli. This is an animal that purposefully uses its behavior to

---

[41] Nor do they visit casinos to gamble and, yet, one could use a Skinner box with five nose poke holes to have rats play the famous *Iowa Gambling Task* (see Zeeb, Robbins, & Winstanley, 2009).

get the most from what its environment has to offer. The studies discussed in the next chapter will further reinforce this notion.

CHAPTER 5: THINKING OUT OF THE BOX

The studies discussed in the previous chapter, which showed how rats can master causal reasoning tasks and assess their own knowledge (metacognition), were performed using the Skinner box. It is interesting (and quite ironic too) to note that this experimental device, originally a symbol of radical behaviorism, is now providing us with cutting-edge evidence of the rat's cognitive processes. But, one might wonder, are the rat's cognitive skills restricted to the artificial environment of the Skinner box? How representative are those studies of a rat's mental life, anyway? In other words, is it possible that the challenges posed by this device can somehow force the animal to go beyond the purely mechanistic or S-R processes in their production of behavior? In the present chapter, I briefly explore several independent lines of research showing that the rat seems to have a pretty busy mental life outside the box as well.

THE MEMORY MAZE

Mazes have a long history in the psychology laboratory. As the reader might remember from Chapter 2, the first psychological experiment ever using albino rats was performed in a maze modeled after the Hampton Court Palace[1]. By the time the widespread use of the maze in the animal laboratory declined due to the increasing popularity of the Skinner box, a large amount of research had already been conducted using mazes, including the studies that

---

[1] Small (1901).

inspired the first cognitive account of spatial navigation in the rat[2].

It is now widely accepted that the rat's ability to find its way in a maze, far from being the result of a series of automatic responses (for example, "turn left" or "turn right") elicited by specific stimuli in the maze (the traditional S-R account), is based on a sort of mental representation that the animal forms of its environment – a cognitive map. But a detailed cognitive map of the maze, as useful as it can be in order to effectively navigate it, is not enough to explain the rat's choice of behavior in the maze on any given moment. A mental map could be tremendously useful if two or more alternative paths could be followed in order to reach a single destination (for example, a goal box containing food). For instance, such a mental map would allow the animal to estimate the relative path lengths at the choice point and, thus, take the shortest path, thereby saving precious time and energy. But what if, at the choice point, the rat had to "decide" between different paths leading to separate destinations containing different food types? Although a cognitive map is still a necessary condition for efficient performance in this latter scenario, it no longer suffices: now the animal's choice will also be determined by the relative value of the alternative food types (for example, palatability and caloric properties). And what if not all of the goal boxes had food continuously available, that is, what if there were temporal constraints on food availability? Certainly, this information should also play a role in the animal's "decision" at the choice point. You see, a rat's life (even a laboratory rat's life) can be quite complex too.

The above scenario might seem artificially overcomplicated, but it is precisely the challenge faced by most wild animals in their daily search for food. In addition to encoding information about

---

[2] Tolman (1948).

their physical environments in the form of cognitive maps, efficient foraging requires learning and remembering exactly where and when a specific kind of food can be found. One well-studied foraging behavior is that of hummingbirds[3], which can visit hundreds of flowers on a single day in their search for nectar. In order to efficiently forage for nectar, these birds must not only remember the location of the flowers, but also keep track of the flowers that have been recently visited, since flowers already visited are temporarily depleted of nectar and, hence, not worth visiting until nectar replenishes (at least 4 hours since the last visit).

Hummingbirds are not alone among birds in their flexible use of information during foraging. A corvid species, the scrub jay, has recently proven to be an expert in this matter. In a highly influential experiment by Clayton and Dickinson[4], scrub jays were given the opportunity to cache (that is, store in a protected or hidden way) and later recover different types of food (for example, peanuts and wax worms) in different locations in one or more trays[5]. Because scrub jays prefer wax worms over peanuts, one would expect that, when given the chance to recover previously cached food, these birds would first dig for the worms. In fact, this is what happens, but only when the jays expect the worms to be fresh and tasty at the time of recovery. In one of the experimental conditions (Degrade), the birds were given the opportunity to learn that worms decayed over time (they were surreptitiously replaced with decayed worms by the experimenters). In this condition, the birds chose to search for worms over peanuts when tested after a 4-hour interval (when

---

[3] See Healy and Hurly (1995).

[4] Clayton and Dickinson (1998). Babb and Crystal (2005) offer a comprehensive summary of the extensive research conducted by Clayton and her collaborators.

[5] Although not central to the present discussion, it is interesting to note that, in order to chache and later retrieve food, an animal requires the ability to represent the continued existence of objects that are not directly available to the senses – an ability known as *object permanence* (Piaget, 1937/1954).

they expected the worms to still be fresh), but reversed their choice when tested after a 124-hour interval (when they expected the worms to be already decayed). A similar result was found in another condition (Pilfer), in which they were trained to expect that previously cached worms would disappear after a long interval of time (they were surreptitiously removed by the experimenters)[6]. As in the Degrade condition, in the Pilfer condition the birds inspected the worm location less when tested after a 124-hour interval than after a 4-hour interval, a result that indicates that they expected the worms to be gone after a long time interval. (However, contrary to the results of the Degrade condition, in the Pilfer condition the preference for worms over peanuts was not reversed after a 124-hour interval, it merely disappeared.) The results of the Degrade and Pilfer conditions cannot be attributed to forgetting, since a third condition (Replenish) had fresh worms continuously available, and the birds in this condition had no problem remembering where to search for worms after either a 4-hour or a 124-hour interval.

These studies with hummingbirds and scrub jays are of great importance since they suggest that these animals might have a memory for specific events, a memory that contains personal and unique experiences. This type of memory, known as *episodic-like memory* (in reference to human episodic memory, but playing it safe with the *-like* suffix since there is no way to assess subjective experiences in nonhuman animals), involves knowledge of *what*, *where*, and *when*. Our episodic memories are the memories of our own lives. We remember ourselves doing certain things (what), in certain places (where), and at specific times (when). The previous studies with scrub jays meet these three criteria: their accurate performance implies that they correctly remember the type food

---

[6] The treatment in the Pilfer condition, as that of the Degrade condition, can be considered naturalistic, since in the wild cached food is typically stolen by other animals, including conspecifics.

they stored (what) in specific locations (where), and how long ago (when)[7].

Inspired by the research conducted by Clayton and Dickinson with the scrub jays, Babb and Crystal[8] more recently conducted a series of studies to assess whether rats also seem to possess episodic-like memory. In their experiments, an 8-arm radial maze was used to evaluate the rat's memory of the specific location of certain foods, as well as their temporal availability (the what-where-when trinity). During the study phase, the rats were given a forced-choice trial on which only 4 of the 8 arms contained food. Specifically, one of the arms contained grape-flavored pellets, another had raspberry-flavored pellets, and the remaining two arms where baited with chow-flavored pellets (the available arms and the specific type of food in each arm were randomly chosen).

After the study phase, a test phase was carried out. This phase could take place after either a short or a long retention interval (1 or 6 hours, respectively). When testing took place after a short retention interval, the 4 arms that were unavailable during the study phase were now made available filled with chow-flavored food. Thus, all 8 arms were now available (free-choice trials), but only the 4 arms that were never visited during the study phase now contained food. As with testing after a short retention interval, when testing was conducted after a long retention interval, the 4 arms made unavailable during the study phase were baited with chow-flavored pellets. Additionally, on test trials after a long retention interval, the grape-flavored and raspberry-flavored pellets were made available again in the exact same arms in which they

---

[7] In the experiments with hummingbirds, only one type of food (nectar) was available. Although nothing precluded learning about the specific quality of the food in these experiments, this learning cannot be categorically asserted. Thus, it can be claimed that these experiments do not necessarily meet the *what* criterion for episodic-like memory.

[8] Babb and Crystal (2006). Also see Babb and Crystal (2005) for a similar, but slightly less sophisticated, study.

were located during the study phase.

Study phase

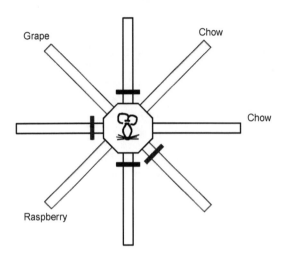

Graphical representation of Babb and Crystal's (2006) experimental design during the study phase.

The rats were repeatedly exposed to daily sessions containing a study phase and a test phase, either after a short or a long retention interval. Given the rats' natural preference for fruity flavors, and assuming that they learned that grape and raspberry pellets would be available again following a long retention interval in the same places where they found them earlier in the day, one would expect the rats to selectively revisit first the arms of the maze containing these fruity pellets. In fact, this result was found. Also, when testing was conducted following a short retention interval, the probability of revisiting any of the arms previously containing grape or raspberry flavors was fairly low.

Test phase – Short retention interval

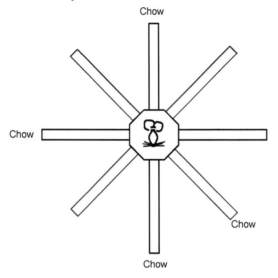

Test phase – Long retention interval

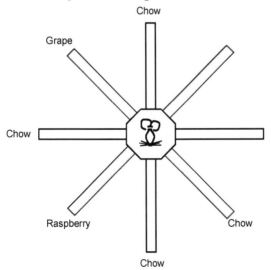

Graphical representation of Babb and Crystal's (2006) experimental design during the test phase after a short retention interval (top panel) and test phase after a long retention interval (bottom panel).

But this is not all. Not only did the animals revisit the arms containing grape and raspberry pellets at comparably high rates on the test following the long retention interval, they also seemingly knew what specific flavor to expect in each arm. When the experimenters devalued one of these two distinctive flavors (devaluation was achieved through satiation, that is, feeding the animals with either grape-flavored or raspberry-flavored pellets between the study and test phases), the probability of a revisit for the devalued flavor decreased (although this difference fell short of statistical significance). In a second part of this experiment, the grape and raspberry pellets were replaced with chocolate and banana pellets. Again, the rats remembered the exact locations of these preferred foods and revisited their corresponding arms more frequently after the long retention interval, but not after the short retention interval. As with the treatment involving satiation-mediated devaluation of either grape or raspberry, one of the new flavors (chocolate) was devalued; only this time devaluation was achieved by pairing the consumption of chocolate-flavored pellets with gastrointestinal illness caused by a LiCl injection. Following this treatment, the visits to the arm containing chocolate, but not to the arms containing the non-devalued flavor (banana) were almost completely discontinued on the tests following a long retention interval.

It is easy to see how closely these findings by Babb and Crystal with rats parallel those of Clayton and Dickinson with scrub jays. In both cases, it is evident that the animal has formed an episodic-like memory containing at least three elements: what (type of food), where (location in the tray or arm in the maze), and when (time since previous cache or lunch). Theoretically, the implications of these studies are deep. Contrary to the other type of declarative memory, namely, semantic memory (theoretical and abstract knowledge unrelated to our personal experiences), episodic memory includes a registry of personal experiences. Thus, making use of this kind of memory implies "traveling back to our own past" (obviously, not to the past *per se*, but to a reconstructed version of the past experiences registered in our brain). It also implies being able to "travel to the future", by mentally simulating future episodes on the basis of previous experience. In other words, it implies what is known as *mental time travel.*[9] Contrary to the popular belief, not all animals are "stuck" in the present. Rather, they seem to be capable of traveling (mentally) in time, just as we do. Another long-held assumption about the special status of *Homo sapiens* in the animal kingdom, proved wrong thanks to recent research in comparative cognition.

In addition to their theoretical implications, these experiments might provide important advances in the understanding and treatment of memory pathologies, such as Alzheimer's disease. This is especially true for Babb and Crystal's research with rats, given that the rat has traditionally been, and still is, a standard subject in psychological and neurological studies, including those studies aiming to understand the determinants of psychological pathologies.

RUNNIN' DOWN A DREAM

As any dog owner can attest (myself included), dreaming is not a uniquely human activity. Dogs usually bark and "run" in dreams, just like we speak (or mumble) and move around in our beds. If you have seen a dog dreaming, you might not be surprised to learn that rats dream too. Interestingly, like dogs and humans, rats also seem to dream about their awake activities.

This is what Wilson and his collaborators[10] found in two separate studies analyzing neural activity in the hippocampus during

---

[9] See Clayton, Bussey, and Dickinson (2003).

[10] Louie and Wilson (2001), Lee and Wilson (2002).

the rapid-eye movement (REM) and the slow-wave (or non-REM) phases of sleep. In these studies, brief segments of awake experience of the rat in a simple maze were then "replayed" (that is, the neural activity was reproduced) by the hippocampus while the animal was sleeping. Also, the replays were substantially different in the slow-wave and REM sleep stages. During slow-wave sleep, the replays were somehow "compressed", with the memory track being played back in just milliseconds, whereas during the REM sleep the memory was played back in almost real time. Moreover, the slow-wave sleep replay only occurred immediately following the awake experience, whereas the REM sleep replay typically occurred 24 hours after the original awake experience, a result that the authors interpreted as suggesting a role in storage of new memories during slow-wave sleep replays and of retrieval of old memories during REM sleep replays.

In addition to the importance of these findings with regard to our understanding of the relation between sleeping/dreaming and the formation of memories, these replays of memories corresponding to awake experiences constitute genuine evidence of the rat's ability to form and store episodic-like memories.

TIT-FOR-RAT

Psychological research using rats has typically assessed the interactions of the animals with their physical environment, namely a Skinner box or a maze. Rats, however, are social animals and it thus makes sense to expect a degree of sophistication in their ability to think about other conspecifics (individuals of the same species). Although comparatively scarce, research has also been conducted in this matter. Only recently, however, have questions about rat social cognition been asked. At first, experiments were performed in the animal conditioning tradition and, accordingly, they aimed to explore the rat's social behavior within the conditioning framework. For example, these experiments sought to extend the domain of classically conditioned stimuli given to a rat from lights and tones to the very presence of another rat or another rat's behavior. In an experiment[11] rats were given the presentation of a rat paired with food, resulting in "pro-social" conditioned responses to the "rat stimulus", such as approach and sniffing, as well as social contact. That is, the pairing of a conspecific with an appetitive outcome (food) resulted in appetitive responses towards the conspecific, but not necessarily the responses unconditionally elicited by food itself (for example, biting, gnawing, swallowing)[12].

In another experiment[13], rats were given footshocks while being exposed to another rat, which was being shocked as well. Although rats normally showed an unconditioned depression in responding (bar pressing for food) when first exposed to another rat being shocked, this reaction to the pain of a conspecific quickly vanished. However, after being exposed to a shocked rat while being shocked themselves (pairings of the pain of a conspecific with their own pain), the animals developed strong fear to the fear of a conspecific[14]. It was thus suggested that *sympathetic* responses to the emotional responses of others are nothing but conditioned responses learned when the emotional responses of other individuals are paired with our own emotional responses[15].

---

[11] Timberlake and Grant (1975).

[12] It is easy to see how this also applies to humans. We have positive feelings towards people who are paired with nice events (for example, playing, laughter, loving and/or sexual contact), and we accordingly approach them and spend more time with them, whereas we tend to avoid people paired with noxious events (for example, stress, boredom, or pain).

[13] Church (1959).

[14] These rats would certainly agree with Franklin D. Roosevelt's famous quote: "The only thing we have to fear is fear itself."

[15] Note that this notion of *sympathy* does not require that the emotions of observed and observer match. Thus, alternative possibilities can be anticipated, such as the conditioning of appetitive responses (for example, pleasure) to another individual's pain, or *vice versa*, the conditioning of aversive responses (for example, fear) to another individual's joy.

In other studies, the reactions of other rats played the role of a US, instead of a CS. Specifically, in these experiments[16] rats housed in pairs were first given access to a flavored solution. Then one of the rats in each pair was made sick (for example, by means of a LiCl injection). As a result, the poisoned partner developed a conditioned aversion to the flavored solution. And, more interestingly, the unpoisoned rat rejected this solution as well[17].

As interesting as these studies are, they do not speak of the rat's social nature. Rather, in these studies rats play the role of CSs or USs for other rats, instead of the role of individuals with which meaningful interactions can be maintained[18]. Recent research by Rutte and Taborsky[19] has brought a fresh perspective on the laboratory rat by asking questions that previously belonged to the primatologists' agenda. Specifically, this research seeks to understand cooperative behavior or reciprocal altruism in the rat. The experimental method can be summarized as follows. First, female rats[20] were trained to pull a stick fixed to a platform to bring it closer to the cage and, thereby, be able to reach a reward (one oat flake) resting on the platform. This training was intended to

---

[16] Lavin, Freise, and Coombes, S. (1980), also see Coombes, Revusky, and Lett (1980).

[17] While the aversion to the flavored solution established for the poisoned rat can be easily explained based on the direct pairing of the solution with the emetic, explaining the unpoisoned rat's aversion requires of more elaborated hypothesis. For example, Coombes and cols. (1980) proposed that the "poisoned partner" effect was due to a pheromone being released by the poisoned rat, which in turn acted as an aversive US for the unpoisoned rat, thereby also resulting in aversive conditioning to the flavored solution for the latter animal.

[18] Obviously, there is a gray area in between these two extremes. For example, Galef and his collaborators (for a review, see Galef, 1996) have extensively studied the social learning component of food preferences in rats, which seems to be related to the smell of food on the breath of a conspecific. This is a very efficient manner of skipping a potentially dangerous food sampling process: if another individual's mouth smells like certain food, that food might probably be safe, so it might be worth trying it.

[19] See Rutte and Taborsky (2007, 2008).

[20] According to the authors of these studies, female rats were used because they are more egalitarian than males, which are more attentive to hierarchy.

facilitate the subsequent training, in which rats were placed into the cage in pairs, separated by a wire mesh panel. During this phase, one of the rats had the opportunity to pull the stick and, thereby, give the other rat access to the reward. Within each couple, the roles of donor and receiver were interchanged repeatedly, so that rats learned to cooperatively work for each other. Subsequent to this pre-experimental training, rats were given the target experimental treatment. In one of the studies[21], the target rats were alternatively exposed to either helping partners or nonhelping partners (nonhelping partners had received no prior training in pulling the stick, but as a precaution the platform was locked and could not be moved). At test, the target rats were in charge of the stick (potential donors) while being introduced to a brand new partner. The authors hypothesized that rats would more likely help the new partner after having received help from other rats, relative to after having received no help. The results supported their predictions, indicating that rats are capable of *generalized reciprocity* (more likely to help a new individual after having received help). These results, the authors claim, resemble those of human research in which people who had previously been helped are more prone to help strangers[22].

In a follow-up experiment[23], the study of reciprocity in rats was extended to the most traditional type, namely, *direct reciprocity* (selectively helping a partner from whom help had been received

---

[21] Rutte and Taborsky (2007).

[22] For example, having found a coin in the coin return of a public phone (studies obviously conducted before everyone had a cell phone) makes one more likely to help a stranger pick up papers that had been accidentally dropped. Unfortunately, pure generalized reciprocity is so unusual in our society that, when it happens, it even appears in the news (see, for example, http://tinyurl.com/36n2te, http://tinyurl.com/cznt8j, http://tinyurl.com/nsy2y2). The movie *Pay it forward* was also inspired in this rare, yet wonderful behavior (see http://www.imdb.com/title/tt0223897).

[23] Rutte and Taborsky (2008).

before), a strategy also known as *reciprocal altruism* or *tit-for-tat*[24]. In a first experiment, the target rats alternatively received help from one partner (cooperator) and no help from another partner (defector). During testing, the target rats were in the donor position (it could choose whether to pull the stick to provide the reward to the partner), and was separately exposed to the cooperator and the defector. The results showed that the target rats were more likely to pull the stick for the cooperator than for the defector, thereby showing that the rat is capable of direct reciprocity. In a second experiment, direct and generalized reciprocity were contrasted. Here, target rats were either presented at test with the same rat that previously helped during training (direct reciprocity) or with a new rat after having received help from different rats (generalized reciprocity). The target rats more often pulled the stick for a known helper than for an unknown individual. In other words, direct reciprocity was found to be stronger than generalized reciprocity.

As acknowledged by the authors of these studies, although direct reciprocity might seem to us simpler than generalized reciprocity, in reality it is more costly in terms of cognitive resources. This is so because direct reciprocity requires the ability to tell apart individuals, as well as good memory for a list of past partners and their interactions (which individuals were previously partners, and whether they helped or not). A species lacking these requirements would be certainly unable to reciprocate directly, but could still reciprocate generally. All generalized reciprocity takes is a simple rule: if you have been recently helped, then help. Despite their modest memory storage capacity compared to that of primates, rats are capable of managing a short list of cooperators and act accordingly (direct reciprocity). When such individual-specific information is not available, however, they seem to help

---

[24] For an evolutionary account of this behavior, see Trivers (1971), and Axelrod and Hamilton (1981).

based on whether they have recently received help (generalized reciprocity). This research promises to bring very interesting future findings[25].

THE DARK SIDE OF SOCIAL NATURE

Rats, as any other social animal, might tremendously benefit from group living. For example, group living provides the group members with protection from predators, opportunity to work cooperatively (reciprocity), as well as multiple opportunities for observational learning (learning from the consequences of a conspecific's behavior). But group living does not come for free in nature. Social species face challenges unknown to solitary species, such as competition with conspecifics for resources such as food and water, mates (male rats compete for females, a behavior that is common of most birds and mammals, including humans[26]), and space to inhabit.

Competition for real estate is much more important than it might seem[27] since, in nature, territory correlates with other resources, such as food and water, thereby improving chances of survival, while also attracting mates. But, what if food, water, and potential mates were guaranteed to everyone in the group and, yet, real estate was still scarce? In other words, what are the consequences of an extremely high population density or overcrowding? This was the question asked by Calhoun in his study

---

[25] And this research is keeping the promise. A few months ago, an article was published which reported the rat's ability to play the Prisoner's Dilemma, a game that involves different rewards and/or punishments as a function of the choice (cooperation vs. defection) of two individuals (see Viana, Gordo, Sucena, & Moita, 2010).

[26] Competition among males for females is not universal in the animal kingdom. In some species (for example, some fishes and birds), females fiercely compete for males.

[27] Enough to kill... even for chimps (Mitani, Watts, & Amsler, 2010).

with rats (later continued with mice)[28], and the results were quite chilling: increased mortality, lowered fertility rates, babies neglected by their mothers, increased aggressive and "psychotic" behavior.

Once again, a parallel emerges between rats and humans. Many of us spend a huge part of our lives in large cities, surrounded by millions of others individuals. Even if we are among the lucky ones whose refrigerator never runs out of food, we will still need to compete for some space in the metro or freeway, in the line at the supermarket, or in the theater[29]. We will also suffer the consequences of the behavior of other people, such as the pollution (including noise) that they generate. Increased population density will inevitably result, as in Calhoun's experiment with rats, in conflict, aggression, and psychological disorders (for example, anxiety and depression). Ironically, contrary to Calhoun's rats, some of us are voluntarily choosing to live in these unbearable conditions.

SIGHS AND LAUGHTER

A social animal could greatly benefit from a communication system. Even if simple, such system would greatly enhance the chances of survival for individuals living in a group. Take, for example, alarm calls in primates, such as those that have been observed in vervet monkeys[30]. The survival value of these calls is obvious: those individuals correctly responding to predator-specific calls (for example, by climbing trees after hearing the "leopard alarm" or jumping out of trees after hearing the "eagle alarm") will be more likely to survive. As for those individuals who make the

---

[28] Calhoun (1962). Also see Galle, Gove, and McPherson (1972) for implications in humans.

[29] Competition for the right of way or a parking spot is a natural (ridiculous though) consequence of our urban/suburban lifestyle.

[30] See Seyfarth, Cheney, and Marler (1980).

calls, their immediate benefit might not be as obvious. First, they have already spotted the predator, so they do not really need to be warned. And second, by making the call they could potentially unveil their position, putting themselves at risk. However, this might be a risk worth taking for an individual living in a group, because she might not always be the first to spot the predator and might also benefit from having other individuals alerting her in the future (that is, reciprocal altruism). Moreover, because some members of the group are likely to be relatives of the individual making the call, this behavior would increase the chances of survival of genetically-related individuals (that is, kin selection).

Social communication systems in nonhuman animals greatly vary in complexity, and certainly none can be comparable to the grammatically intricate languages spoken by *Homo sapiens*. Nevertheless, their importance in terms of adaptation (enhanced likelihood of survival and reproduction) should not be dismissed. It thus makes sense to expect a social animal like the rat to be able to use some sort of social communication system involving not just smells[31], but also sounds. As a matter of fact, recent evidence of two types of sounds with a presumed communicative function have been observed in the rat.

One of these two sounds is a "sigh", a respiratory event well known to humans. Interestingly, as in the case of the human sigh ("sigh of relief"), this event seems to correlate with relief in rats, as revealed by a study by Soltysik and Jelen[32]. Relief, for humans, can be defined as the feeling associated with the removal of fear, stress, or discomfort. In an experiment with rats, such feeling of relief can be induced in the animal each time an expected noxious event is not

---

[31] As in the previously mentioned cases of food preference learning (smell of food in a conspecific's mouth) and the "poisoned partner" (a pheromone released by the poisoned rat).

[32] Soltysik and Jelen (2005).

actually presented. This is the case of the experimental treatment known as *Pavlovian conditioned inhibition*, in which pairings of a CS (for example, a light) with the US (for example, footshock) are interspersed with presentations of the CS in compound with another CS (for example, a tone) in the absence of the US. After several light-shock pairings are intermixed with light+tone compound presentations (without the shock), the light elicits a fear response (it becomes a predictor of the occurrence of shock), which can be counteracted or inhibited by the presentation of the tone (it becomes a predictor of the nonoccurrence of shock). Interestingly, not only does the tone counteract the fear response otherwise produced by the light, but it also evokes responses that are antagonistic to fear, such as relaxation[33] or relief. Such feeling of relief seems to correlate with the respiratory event that the authors of this study referred to as a sigh, with a presumed communicative value:

> *The "ultimate cause" might be that this respiratory act was recruited during evolution to signal reduced perception of danger and/or to synchronise (collective sighs of relief?) the emotional state of the group of conspecifics. In other words, [...] sighs are rat's expression of relief, and as such could function as social signals of safety. The sigh could be a signal opposite to the alarm cry.*[34]

As for the expression of more joyful feelings, it seems that rats can laugh as well. At least, such is the view of Panksepp, the author of an extensive line of research[35] attempting to find an animal model (with rats) of human joy. The rat's "laughter" consists of an ultrasonic vocalization of 50-kHz, which is abundant while playing with conspecifics and, even more, when being tickled by a

---

[33] See Denny (1971).

[34] Soltysik and Jelen (2005), p. 601.

[35] For a review, see Panksepp and Burgdorf (2003).

human. The authors compare these 50-kHz chirps to the genuine laughter of human children. As in humans, in rats the "laughter chirps" are produced more often by youngsters, both when playing and when being tickled (adult rats play less and seem to laugh less when tickled). In support to their view of these 50-kHz chirps being indicative of a positive affect (akin to what we know as "joy" or "mirth"), the authors comment on studies showing the classical conditioning of appetitive responses with tickling as the US. Rats that have been tickled tend to approach the hands that tickled them, and show a marked preference for the place in which they were tickled. Also, they seem to initiate social solicitations (play-bites) as a "request" for tickles. Being tickled also seems to work as a powerful instrumental reward, since rats can be trained to run mazes or press levers just for the sake of getting a tickle. However, just as we do, rats can find excessive tickling aversive, with the 50-kHz chirps being eventually replaced by 22-kHz (a sound typically emitted in affectively negative situations).

A RAT'S LIFE… JUST GETS COMPLICATED

In the present chapter I have discussed a few "unconventional" lines of research using rats as subjects. We have seen that rats not only learn their way around mazes, but also seem to have a good (episodic-like) memory of their personal experiences in it. We have also seen that rats seem to dream about their awake activities (such as running the maze) while sleeping. Rats are also capable of both direct and generalized reciprocity, feats that until recently were thought to be achieved only by primates. Finally, we have seen that rats seem to sigh in relief (when an expected shock does not happen) and laugh when playing with other rats or when tickled by humans. This chapter (if effectively achieving its goal) should leave the reader with the impression, if not the conviction, that a rat's behavior is much more than the mechanistic universe of radical behaviorism. A rat's life seems to be more complicated than we could ever imagine, and it is getting even more complicated as more publications shed light on the inner life of this animal.

CHAPTER 6: WHY SHOULD A RAT THINK ANYWAY?

In the previous chapters, I discussed the results of experiments conducted in the area of animal learning and comparative cognition over the last few years, which I considered to be indicative of sophisticated cognitive processes in the rat. In other words, although arguable (especially to those in the behaviorist tradition) these studies indicate that the rat is an intelligent animal capable of thinking. But, the reader might wonder, why should a rat think anyway? What is the point of possessing relatively complex mental capabilities for an animal like the rat, with such a simple way of life? After all, it is not like they have to search for jobs, learn one or more languages, deal with algebra at school, or drive a car to buy the groceries. So, what is it? What is thinking all about? The reason behind thinking is much simpler than that, and more important too. It is about life and death. And it is about sex too or, more precisely, the product thereof: making babies.

A VERY DARWINIAN LIFE

In 1859, Charles Darwin published his book *On the origin of species by means of natural selection, or the preservation of favoured races in the struggle for life* (commonly known as *On the origin of species* for obvious reasons), a book that changed forever our understanding of biological evolution (the change in a population's inherited traits from generation to generation), propelling natural science to a higher level while inflicting a deadly wound to the creationist account of human existence[1].

---

[1] In fact, the real mess between supporters of evolutionary theory (such as Thomas

(Footnote continued on next page)

In his *On the origin of species*, Darwin proposed a simple, yet powerful theory of evolution[2], a theory that, as of today, still remains unchallenged. This theory, known as *natural selection*, is nicely summarized in the introduction of the book:

> *As many more individuals of each species are born than can possibly survive; and as, consequently, there is a frequently recurring struggle for existence, it follows that any being, if it vary however slightly in any manner profitable to itself, under the complex and sometimes varying conditions of life, will have a better chance of surviving, and thus be naturally selected. From the strong principle of inheritance, any selected variety will tend to propagate its new and modified form.*[3]

Huxley, *aka* "Darwin's Bulldog") and religious advocates of creationism worsened after the publication of *The descent of man, and selection in relation to sex*, in 1871. The reader interested in the battle between evolution vs. creation (or intelligent design, in its latest rebrand) should consider the following books: Dawkins (2006), Miller (2008), Scott (2005), Shermer (2006).

[2] Two common misunderstandings about the expression "theory of evolution" need to be pointed out. First, this expression does not mean that evolution is a theory, as creationists and intelligent design advocates like to believe. Evolution is a fact that has been established from multiple sources (for example, fossil record, the geographical distribution of species, and molecular genetics, to name a few). In fact, evolution was already established as a fact in the scientific community prior to Darwin's work: Jean-Baptiste Lamarck had already produced his theory of inheritance of acquired traits to explain evolution, a theory that was abandoned when Darwin proposed natural selection as the mechanism operating in evolution. Even Darwin's grandfather, Erasmus Darwin, wrote about evolution. Darwin proposed natural selection (a theory) as an account of biological evolution (a fact).

Second, Darwin proposed no more, no less, a theory of evolution. However, in science a theory is not just a vague idea or a guess. (It took Darwin more than 20 years to publish his theory since he originally conceived it during his voyage in HSM *Beagle*, from 1831 to 1836.) A scientific theory, such as Darwin's, is the product of a long line of work that starts with gathering and analyzing data (using observational, correlational, or experimental techniques) in order to assess hypothesis, and that ends with the formulation of an organized explanation of evidence (the theory). That is, a scientific theory is produced within the constraints established by the scientific method. Because of this, scientific theories are accepted or rejected by the scientific community exclusively based on their ability to provide a comprehensive account of known evidence. Whether the scientists dislike or disagree with the theory is not enough to reject it. Only new scientifically collected evidence, if strong enough, can expel a leading theory from its throne.

[3] This text can be found on p. 23 of the 1909 edition of *On the origin of species* (New York: P. F. Collier & Son), available for download in PDF at Google books.

In other words, Darwin's theory of evolution proposes the concurrent operation of two simple mechanisms, namely, variation and natural selection. *Variation* naturally occurs during reproduction. Such variation is guaranteed due to the genetic shuffling that occurs during *meiosis*, or the production of reproductive cells (gametes for animals, and spores for other organisms, such as plants, fungi, algae, bacteria, and protozoans). In organisms that reproduce sexually, the shuffling goes even further given that the individual's genetic makeup is the result of a unique mix of the genes from each parent (with father and mother contributing equally with 50% of their genes of their offspring[4]). Moreover, variation can be introduced during reproduction due to random genetic mutations, or "errors" in the replication or copying of the DNA sequence in the production of the reproductive cells.

The *gene*, or unit of inheritance that is passed on to the next generation, is nowadays intimately ingrained in our understanding of evolution. But Darwin never knew of the role that genes play the inheritance of traits. He was never aware of Gregor Mendel's original studies in genetics with pea plants, even when these studies were performed during his lifetime (in the 1860s), and the molecular structure of DNA was discovered by Crick, Watson, and Franklin[5] in 1953 (long after Darwin's death, in 1882). Nevertheless, it was well known in Darwin's time that traits were somehow passed on to the next generation, according to "the strong principle of inheritance" to which Darwin refers in the previous quote.

The second process is *natural selection*, which merely means

---

[4] By "genes", here I refer to *alleles*, or alternative forms of a gene. Alleles are genes that occupy the same place or *locus* in different homologous chromosomes, thereby controlling the same trait (for example, two genes in charge of determining the color of the eyes are alleles for each other).

[5] Watson and Crick received the Nobel Prize in Physiology or Medicine in 1962 for this discovery along with Wilkins. Unfortunately, Franklin's contribution was not acknowledged at the time.

that individuals with those traits that allow them to fit into their environments will have more chances of survival and, thus, of reproduction. Therefore, those individuals with advantageous traits (the *fittest* individuals) have more chances of reproducing and, thus, of passing on their traits to the next generation. Therefore, over time, this process results in organisms that are progressively better adapted to their environments. Thus, it could be said that different environments shape, generation after generation, the inheritable traits of those species that dwell in them. A species' environment not only consists of the ecological area or physical location (its *habitat*). It includes other species as well, species that might be interesting for the organism as food (prey) or interested in the organism as food (predator), species that might compete with the organism for the same source of food, and species that share the organism's habitat without much interference. Finally, an organism's environment might include other conspecifics as well, especially for social species. Competition among individuals within a species will be ensured when resources (for example, food, water, space) are scarce. All these environmental pressures define the organism's *ecological niche*, that is, its lifestyle within its ecosystem.

And, yet, that is not all. Add to all this competition for mates, which in many species (for example, most mammals and birds) takes the form of competition among males for females, and the picture just gets more complicated. This struggle to make babies is an important evolutionary force, known as *sexual selection*[6]. In fact, it is so important that it sometimes might result in the evolution of traits that, although extremely useful for the purpose of attracting the other sex, can be disadvantageous for survival. Take, for example, the beautiful display of colors in the plumage of the peacock. As irresistible as it might be for the peahen, this plumage is an open invitation, almost a living billboard, to potential

---

[6] Darwin (1871).

predators. Sexual selection results in *sexual dimorphism*, or appreciable differences between males and females from the same species, such as different sizes, colors (typical in birds), or even body parts exclusive to one of the sexes (for example, ornamental feathers, horns, and antlers, typically used as tools for sexual competition, be it for courting the females or for fighting with other males to deter them from courting the females).

Natural selection not only produces better adapted organisms, it can also create new species. This phenomenon, known as *speciation*, can happen when a population of organisms from the same species splits into separate geographical locations. As a consequence, each subpopulation will be subject to different environmental pressures, to which they will progressively adapt (the alternative being the decease of all members of the subpopulation, that is, *extinction*)[7]. Because different traits can be advantageous in each of these separate environments, differences will arise between these subpopulations. Eventually, these differences will become so deep that these subpopulations will no longer be able to interbreed or, in other words, that they belong to separate species.

Current understanding of evolution and natural selection differs slightly from Darwin's in that selection does not operate at the level of the individual, as posited by Darwin, but at the level of the genes. Richard Dawkins' *selfish gene* theory[8] is a great example of this viewpoint. According to Dawkins, genes build organisms or, in his own words, *survival machines*. Only successful genes build successful organisms in the struggle for survival, organisms that live long enough to reproduce. That is, only successful genes replicate.

---

[7] Death is not only part of failure (extinction), but also of success (adaptation). The differential survival and reproduction of individuals with adaptive traits necessarily implies that those individuals lacking such traits will fail to live long enough to produce offspring. Thus, even in the best case scenario, a drastic change in the environmental conditions will leave death in its wake.

[8] Dawkins (1976).

Unsuccessful genes are weeded out by natural selection. Genes, according to Dawkins, are selfish in the sense that they only "care" about their own replication (no hard feelings about this, the attribute "selfish" has no negative connotation for genes). This implies that, although the organism's phenotype (observable traits) determines its chances of survival and reproduction, in the end it is the organism's genotype (its genetic makeup) that is selected. As successful as some organisms might be in the game of life, all organisms eventually die, and their evolutionary success is measured in terms of the number of descendants left behind. In other words, what matters is the number of copies of their genes, which reside in the bodies of their offspring.

But natural selection not only designs organisms with bodily structures finely adapted to their environment, it also designs their behaviors, which serve the purpose of survival and reproduction as well. Darwin himself had the foresight to apply his own theory to psychology in his book *The expression of the emotions in man and animals*, first published in 1872, in which he discussed the continuity of behavior from nonhuman animals to humans. Today, evolutionary theory is ubiquitous in psychology, from evolutionary psychology (a hybrid of cognitive psychology and evolutionary theory, with emphasis on the evolutionary origins of human cognition and behavior) to comparative psychology (the study of animal behavior, with emphasis on the similarities and differences among species). This should be no surprise, given that natural selection designs all organs, including the brain and, thus, its wiring and programming – the mind. In other words, natural selection operates on both the hardware (the brain) and the software (the mind). As stated in the famous title of Theodosius Dobzhansky's essay, "Nothing in biology makes sense except in the light of evolution"[9]. The same is true for psychology.

---

[9] Dobzhansky (1973).

LEARNING TO LIVE

Take a second to think of the multiple challenges any given animal might face on a daily basis, challenges such as finding and extracting food, sometimes carrying a portion of that food to its offspring; finding and, quite often, fighting for a partner (one at least, more in polygamous species); avoiding getting too close to potential predators and effectively fleeing from them to avoid becoming lunch, or fiercely fight for its own life or the lives of its offspring.

This rather incomplete checklist of the "duties of life" includes some of the many behaviors that ethologists have thoroughly studied over the last decades since the inaugural research of Konrad Lorenz and Nikolaas Tinbergen in the 1930s. As a brand of zoology and, hence, of biology, ethologists emphasize the role of the genetic determinants of behavior. In other words, they focus on the innate aspects of behavior (they lean towards the nature side of the *nature versus nurture* debate). To the extent that the instructions for behavioral patterns can be encoded in the genes, such behaviors can be inheritable, or passed down to the next generation. These behaviors are what ethologists refer to as *fixed (or modal) action patterns*, or what most people know as *instincts*. Although instincts are typically considered to be relatively simple behavior patterns (for example, herring-gull chicks pecking on the tip of the parent's bill induces regurgitation in the parent, which provides the chick with food), some instincts might sometimes be quite elaborate (for example, the *waggle dance* performed by bees to communicate the location of flowers containing nectar; or some courtship interactions in birds, which include the construction of the nest by both male and female).

It is not hard to see the relevance of instinctive behavior in the game of life. An organism's chances of survival are greatly enhanced by coming to this world with a set of behaviors that have been finely tuned to meet basic environmental demands, a set of behaviors that has been shaped and polished by natural selection over thousands, sometimes millions, of years, generation after generation[10]. But instinctive behavior, as critical as it might be for survival, is rarely enough. Organisms frequently need to adjust their behavior to the demands of their constantly changing environments. Here is where learning enters the game.

Learning, or the ability of an organism to change its behavior based on the multiple interactions with its environment (both physical and social), is as essential for the organism's survival as instinctive behavior. Just like instincts, learning mechanisms are genetically encoded in the organism and are passed down from generation to generation. However, while instincts contain specific instructions involving the responses to be produced in the presence of specific stimuli as well as their sequence, learning mechanisms are detached (not always completely so, though) from the specific stimuli and responses that will be involved in the learning process. In other words, learning mechanisms just contain the basic rules by which stimuli and responses must interact in the learning process.

Take, for example, Thorndike's Law of Effect (discussed in Chapter 2), which states that any response that is followed by a pleasant effect (a reinforcer, in Skinner's terms) will be more likely to occur in the future (will be reinforced or strengthened, in Skinner's terms). Such a law does not speak of the specific responses that can be strengthened, and neither points out which pleasant consequences will have the effect of reinforcing a given response. In fact, its beauty lies in both its simplicity and its generality. The same rule applies equally to any the response-effect combination and all animal species, be it a cat releasing a latch to open the door in a puzzle box, or a dog "begging" for food, or a baby crying for attention and comfort. Similarly to operant

---

[10] Richard Dawkins provides an excellent review of a wide variety of instinctive behaviors in his masterpiece *The selfish gene* (Dawkins, 1976).

conditioning, classical conditioning mechanisms are silent in regards to the specific stimuli entering into an association. From Pavlov's dogs salivating to the sound of a metronome previously paired with food, or to a child reacting with panic to dogs after being bitten by one, the same underlying rule applies.

Instinctive behavior and learning mechanisms complement each other. Instincts provide the individual with a quick "solution" to a simple "problem", a behavior or sequence of behaviors to a stimulus or pattern of stimuli. These behaviors worked in the past for the individual's ancestors and will likely work for this particular individual as well. Learning mechanisms allow the individual to quickly adjust behavior to the idiosyncrasy of the environmental conditions in which such an individual lives. Although both instincts and learning mechanisms are, in fact, complementary, their relative weight or importance varies strongly across species. Simply put, species that dwell in highly changing environments (for example, *Homo sapiens*) rely deeply on learning mechanisms over instinctive behaviors. By contrast, the behavior of species dwelling in pretty stable environments (for example, *Drosophila, aka* the common fruit fly) will be mostly instinctive. This is not to say that we, humans, lack instincts or that fruit flies cannot learn[11]. Rather, this means that behavior is based on both instincts and learning mechanisms, but the relative contribution of nature and nurture varies across species.

Also, far from the original view of instinctive behavior as stereotyped and rigid behavior exclusively dictated by genetic factors, it is now known and widely accepted by ethologists that instincts can be, as a matter of fact, quite flexible and can be tailored by experience (this is the case of the waggle dance in bees). Conversely, learning mechanisms are not completely detached from

---

[11] See De Belle and Heisenberg (1994) for a representative study on learning and memory in *Drosophila*.

the nature of the stimuli and responses that can enter into associations. Rather, these mechanisms incorporate certain constraints, filtering the contents of learning. This is commonly referred to as *preparedness*[12].

As a great example of preparedness, take the ability of migratory birds to make use of constellations as a "compass" when flying overnight. Such information is not genetically encoded. It could not possibly be this way, since the earth's axis rotation and, thus, the celestial pole changes every 27,000 years. As long as 27,000 years might seem, it is too fast in the evolutionary scale: by the time this information could become genetically encoded, it would already be outdated. Learning seems to be a better solution than instinct in this case, but this learning has to be guided somehow, and here is where the genes play a role, by selecting the kind of information these birds pay attention to and, therefore, learn since their earliest days. Nestlings will spend most of their night time watching the rotation of the constellations, learning about them[13].

In the classical conditioning literature, this preparedness typically regards the relation between the conditioned and unconditioned stimuli (CS and US) or, as is commonly referred to, the *CS-US relevance* or *belongingness*. For instance, humans will readily associate pictures of snakes or spiders, but not pictures of flowers or houses, with electric shock[14], a finding that makes perfect sense in light of the great adaptive value of learning to fear snakes and spiders[15]. In a similar vein, rats readily associate a new flavor with

---

[12] Seligman (1971).

[13] This example was borrowed from Pinker (2009), who provides one of the fiercest and most brilliant defenses of evolutionary psychology to the date.

[14] Öhman, Dimberg, and Öst (1985).

[15] Of course, not many of us encounter these "scary" animals frequently in our urban environments. But our brains have not been "crafted" yet by natural selection to the lifestyle of our modern cities. Our brains are tuned to the lifestyle of the Savanna, our

(Footnote continued on next page)

gastrointestinal illness (resulting in conditioned aversion to the flavor), but not with footshock. Conversely, rats readily associate audiovisual stimuli with footshock (resulting in conditioned fear to the audiovisual stimuli), but not with gastrointestinal illness[16]. Again, the adaptive value of such biased learning mechanism is obvious if we consider how, in the wild, these stimuli relate to each other. Gastrointestinal pain normally results from the ingestion of toxic or poisonous substances, which can be identified from their gustatory and olfactory features. That is, internal or interoceptive pain is normally caused by stimuli previously introduced in the organism's system[17]. By contrast, audiovisual stimuli are good predictors of threats that could potentially result in injury or death, such as predators or bad weather. In other words, external or exteroceptive pain is normally caused by stimuli that are external to the organism. It thus makes sense that audiviovisual stimuli are readily learned as reliable predictors of shock, which causes exteroceptive pain. Analogously, pigeons more readily associate visual stimuli with food and auditory stimuli with footshock[18], a finding consistent with the

---

EEA (*Environment of Evolutionary Adaptedness*), the wild environment in which our species dwelt for most of its evolutionary history.

[16] Garcia and Koelling (1966).

[17] Humans are not unlike rats. Life provides us with multiple opportunities to learn to tell apart the things that we can safely eat/drink from those we should stay away from. For example, we can suffer food poisoning (1 out of 5 Americans do so every year) after eating a burger. Or we can feel sick after drinking too much wine. Or we can simply feel nauseated after a wild ride on a roller coaster. In all instances, the taste of the food/drink will likely become aversive, that is, it will elicit conditioned nausea or an emotional reaction of disgust. Most of the time, this response will prevent us from consuming a potentially harmful substance once again, such as the burger or the wine that made us sick. Occasionally though, we might end up avoiding completely inoffensive substances – such as that delicious cotton candy that we ate just before that ride on the roller coaster. Cancer patients undergoing chemotherapy and radiotherapy treatments also learn to associate the foods they ate before their therapy sessions with the illness they subsequently experience, even when they are aware that the foods cannot be blamed for their illness. (Incidentally, chemotherapy and radiotherapy treatments closely parallel illness induced by the injection of LiCl and by exposure to X-rays, respectively, in the animal laboratory.)

[18] Foree and LoLordo (1973).

fact that, in the wild, they forage for food mainly based on visual cues, and avoid predators mainly based on auditory cues. In other words, for pigeons, visual cues are useful for finding food and auditory cues are critical to avoid becoming food.

The above examples indicate that biological preparedness affects classical conditioning. Not surprisingly, the same constraints are known to affect operant conditioning mechanisms. As with the CS-US relationship, the response and the outcome must naturally belong with each other in order for good conditioning to occur. In other words, the outcome must be relevant within the response system in which the operant response is involved. In his original studies with cats, Thorndike observed that certain responses, such as scratching itself or yawning, could not be effectively reinforced with food[19]. In fact, in the wild, these responses do not belong to the feeding system (scratching or yawning are very unlikely to yield food). In their famous publication *The misbehavior of organisms*[20] (a really clever title when one considers that Skinner first laid the foundation of operant conditioning in his book *The behavior of organisms*[21]), the Brelands described their difficulties in teaching different animals (for example, raccoons and pigs) certain operant responses due to the interference caused by the appearance of more naturalistic food-related behaviors (for example, rubbing or rooting the objects associated with the food reward), which they referred to as *instinctive drift*.

There is a thin, blurry line between instincts and learning, between nature and nurture. Instinctive behavior can be tailored by learning, and learning can be guided by innate constraints. In both cases, behavior is finely adapted to the demands of the organism's

---

[19] Domjan (2009).

[20] Breland and Breland (1961).

[21] Skinner (1938).

environment, be it the features of the environment that have remained relatively unchanged for a long period of time (in which case, instinctive behavior might take a predominant role), or the features of the environment that are highly variable (in which case, a learning mechanism able to capture the idiosyncrasy of the organism's environment will be necessary). Differences aside, in both cases, the ultimate goal is to promote the organism's survival and reproduction. In other words, the mechanisms underlying behavior, be it innate or learned, are nothing but an adaptation, a trait that allows the organism to fit in its environment. As I will discuss later on in this chapter, this makes perfect sense when we consider that these mechanisms have been "crafted" the hard way, the way of life or death – the way of natural selection.

THINKING AS AN ADAPTATION

In the previous chapters, I discussed different lines of research that indicate that rats possess the cognitive ability generally referred to as *thinking*. The reader, however, might still remain unconvinced. Sure, rats can do some interesting things we did not know they were capable of, but are those feats representative of what we commonly understand as thinking? What do we mean by thinking anyway? In the layman's language, thinking seems to be almost anything we, humans[22], normally do with our minds (at least consciously). For instance, we use this word to refer to decision making ("you need to think about your future career plans"), believing or being of an opinion ("most scientists think that global warming is a real threat"), guessing ("I think we should take Exit 51"), or remembering ("grandpa was thinking of the old times"),

---

[22] Implicit to this, is the idea that thinking is an exclusively human attribute, which sets us apart from the rest of the animal kingdom. This is nothing else than Cartesian dualism (Descartes, 1637), as applied to *pop psychology* mostly for reasons of religious nature.

imagining ("I can't stop thinking of the day I will move to another place, far-far away from here"), and problem solving ("I need to think this through").

In psychology or, at least, in the animal behavior literature, thinking has a more restrained meaning, and normally refers to a mental process oriented towards problem solving. That is, thinking involves the manipulation of information by the animal in order to solve a problem, thereby achieving a specific goal. As such, thinking might be seen as an adaptation, just like in the case of instinctive behavior and learning mechanisms: to the extent that thinking might allow the animal to more effectively overcome the multiple challenges posed by the environment, it will improve the animal's chances of survival and reproduction.

THINKING... THE RAT WAY

As narrow as the previous definition of thinking might seem, it is still quite multifaceted. By thinking, animal psychologists might refer to the mental processes involved in *insight,* or the sudden realization of a solution to a problem. Thinking might mean causal understanding and causal reasoning, or drawing inferences or conclusions from acquired information about the causal texture of the environment. Thinking is also involved in tool-using and tool-making, as it is in mental simulation (modeling reality in one's mind), an activity that is related to anticipating and planning the future. And, for those species that can afford the required cognitive power, thinking plays a big role in the formation and use of a *theory of mind,* or understanding the minds of other individuals, which involves knowing about the contents of these minds (their knowledge, ideas, beliefs, feelings, hopes, fears, etc.)[23].

---

[23] To the extent that behavior is mostly determined by the contents of the mind, a *theory of mind* allows the animal to make predictions regarding the likely behaviors of other

(Footnote continued on next page)

These facets of what we call thinking have been extensively studied in nonhuman primates (typically great apes, that is, chimpanzees, bonobos, gorillas, and orangutans – although monkeys have received great attention as well)[24], and cetaceans (especially toothed whales or *odontoceti*, which includes the well-known bottlenose dolphin and the orca or *killer whale*). These cognitive abilities are not available to the rat. It would be preposterous to state that the rat possesses intelligence comparable to that of primates or toothed whales. But to deny the rat a little parcel in the realm of intelligence also seems unfair in light of the studies discussed in this book. We have seen that rats are capable of quite sophisticated causal reasoning (Chapter 4), and have the property known as metacognition (Chapter 4). They also seem to be able to remember multiple aspects of their past personal and unique experiences (information regarding *what*, *where*, and *when*), which indicates that they have an episodic-like memory. In turn, this kind of memory might allow rats to mentally travel in time by recreating past events and simulating future events on the basis of previous experiences (Chapter 5). And, when it comes to dealing with conspecifics, they can engage in direct reciprocity (tit-for-tat), which involves keeping a mental list of past helpers in order to determine whether to help in future interactions (Chapter 5). There is, in sum, sufficient evidence in the rat of what we call thinking.

THE MIRROR OF THE BODY... AND THE MIND

It takes no expert to guess in what type of environment an animal species dwells. Give a child a picture of an animal she never knew of before, and she might be able to correctly categorize this

---

individuals or even to manipulate their behaviors by introducing certain bits of information in their minds.

[24] See Byrne (1995) for a good introductory text on ape cognition.

animal as terrestrial or aquatic. She might even tell you if this animal is able to fly or, like us, dwells on firm ground. Likewise, we can tell what an animal likely eats based on some morphological clues. Sharp teeth and relatively large stomach with a short intestinal tract are typical of carnivores (their food must be first caught and killed, but once their flesh has been torn off and swallowed, it is quickly processed); whereas flat teeth and long intestinal tracts with almost no stomach are found in herbivores (their food must be grinded before swallowing, and requires more processing to be broken down and absorbed).

Interestingly, based on this information provided by observation (or careful study) of an animal's anatomy we can infer its likely lifestyle, which obviously implies inferring aspects of its behavior[25]. Someone with an expert eye (for example, a zoologist) will be able to "read" an animal's body like an open book, providing a great deal of insight about its environment and the way this animal dwells in it (its ecological niche), a reading that is possible only because of the lawful relationship existing between environment and body. One such lawful relationship is natural selection, previously described. Generation after generation, animals with bodies that were somehow better adjusted to the demands of the environment were in advantage relative to those with bodies less tuned up to such demands, and were accordingly more likely to survive and reproduce, thereby passing down their traits to the next generation.

Because an animal's body is the cumulative product of all the feats that worked well for its ancestors over a long period of time, this body will necessarily provide us with partial information. First,

---

[25] Of course, this is not a standard procedure in the study of the behavior of live animals. For that shake, direct observation of their behavior will provide with much more, and more reliable information. But this is a standard procedure (among others) when it comes to inferring the likely behavior of a long-gone species. In fact, paleontologists do this just based on a more or less complete collection of fossilized bones.

it will mostly speak of past success, of achievements in the struggle for life (adaptations), being silent regarding the many attempts (for example, mutations) that never worked. Second, given the large amount of time that natural selection requires to operate, it will provide us with somewhat outdated information. This delay might reflect just an instant in the evolutionary timescale (measured in million years), but it certainly matters for the organism that is trying to make it to the end of the day right here and right now: this organism has to deal with its current environment by employing a body that has been shaped (through evolution) to deal with a past environment. To the extent that these environments, current and past, might overlap, old traits might be still useful. But this is not always the case, and fast changing environments will have devastating effects on the survival of the organisms inhabiting them. Anyone who has seen a dried-up river, with its previously thriving fish writhing to catch another breath, can understand this.

Knowing that an animal's body is the product of natural selection can also explain why organisms, as perfectly adapted as they might be to their environments, often have puzzling "flaws" or "useless features" in their design. Natural selection is a really potent designer, but a non-intelligent one. As such, it cannot foresee what kind of conditions organisms will meet in their future environments. Natural selection works on current organisms based on their current conditions. And it works very slowly, chipping away at the poorly adaptive traits on each successive generation. A necessary consequence of natural selection's predilection for success, combined with the fact that it operates over long time periods (compared to our ephemeral lifetime), is that many organisms carry *vestigial traits*. These traits are of no current use for their carrier, but had a function in the organism's ancestry. For example, the vermiform appendix and the wisdom teeth are vestigial traits in humans, the legacy of the herbivorous lifestyle of our ancestors.

Like with its body, an animal's mind (its contents and

processes) can be seen as a transcript of the evolutionary history of its species. Paraphrasing what I previously stated about bodily structures, an animal's mind is the cumulative product of all the feats that worked well for its ancestors over a long period of time. That is, the mind is a finely crafted survival tool. This means that the mind, as the body, must reflect the environmental pressures for which it evolved. While different species dwelling in different ecosystems must necessarily adapt to their specific conditions, it is reasonable to expect all these ecosystems to share a series of common characteristics. After all, we all inhabit the same planet, a planet that is no exception to the universal laws of physics and chemistry. For example, gravity pulls all animals in the same direction (towards the center of our planet) and with the same force (g), making no exception whatsoever. Organisms are also slaves to the first law of thermodynamics (the law of conservation of energy), as well as its extension to the world of matter (the mass-energy equivalence, famously summarized in Albert Einstein's famous equation, $E=mc^2$), although for living things this normally translates in something pretty simple: since bodies are made of matter and all behavior consumes energy, animals need food for their survival.

REASONS FOR REASONING

An animal's intuitive appreciation of gravity or the concept of mass-energy equivalence, as relevant as this might be in the wild (especially for an animal facing the edge of a high cliff or unprecedented famine), is not the kind of mental trait that has attracted the general interest of animal psychologists – at least not yet. The interests of animal psychologists are, in fact, similar to those of psychologists with an interest in standard (human) psychology, which are historically rooted in philosophy. A good example of this is the study of causal learning in humans and nonhuman animals, which can be traced back to David Hume's original discourse on causation[26]. There are strict regularities in the causal texture of our world (actually, they can be presumed to be universal regularities), such as the fact that causes always precede effects, that causes rarely occur without being followed by their effects, and that effects rarely appear without being preceded by their causes[27].

As I already discussed (see Chapter 4), effective causal learning allows an animal to predict the occurrence of an event,

---

[26] Hume (1739/1964).

[27] Needless to say, the situation can be (and usually is) more complex than this, and plenty of studies have been conducted in human contingency learning to understand how we manage to apprehend various complicated scenarios. Simply put, in reality, causes *always* precede effects, but that does not mean that the causal structure of our environment will be clear-cut in all cases. There are several ways in which our intuitive understanding of causal relations could lead to erroneous conclusions. Let us consider here three common sources of error in the detection of causal relations:

An event (Event 1) that regularly precedes another event (Event 2) does not have to necessarily be its cause. In fact, the order could be reversed. A couple of examples will serve to clarify this. For instance, the flashing lights (and the annoying noise that accompanies them) normally precede the presence of a train at a railroad crossing. However, these lights do not cause the appearance of the train. Rather, they are an effect thereof (someone, or a computerized system, activates them when a train is approaching). Similarly, you might always eat pop-corn in the theater while waiting for the movie to start, but eating pop-corn does not cause the start of the movie... it is the anticipation of the movie (and the unarguable truth that pop-corn always makes a movie better), what makes you more likely to eat pop-corn.

Event 1 and Event 2 could be the effects of a third event, which causes them in a serial manner, giving an illusion of causality. For example, after eating poisoned food and falling sick, animals learn to avoid the taste of the food and, thus, the ingestion thereof. In fact, the taste becomes aversive ("yucky") and elicits nausea. This learning is highly valuable for survival, since it serves to prevent the accidental ingestion of a known toxic food in the future (since chances are that the same taste will be accompanied by the same toxin again). However, this does not mean that the taste caused the poisoning. Rather, both the taste and the toxin (the latter being responsible for the illness) are the product of the same plant or animal, and eating this food resulted in the contiguous occurrence of these events, one followed by another: taste first, followed by poisoning.

Event 1 and Event 2 could be totally unrelated from each other but, due to the high frequency of Event 1, combined with our very human tendency to remember the hits (Event 1 followed by Event 2) and forget the misses (Event 1 without Event 2), they seem to be related. This is the case of rain dance in some forager cultures, or praying in our own culture. (More on this later on in this chapter.)

adapting its behavior accordingly (for example, knowing that a noise predicts a snake will elicit a freezing or fleeing response). However, the benefits of causal learning surpass those of predictive learning. Causal learning can also allow the animal to influence the occurrence of events, something that routinely happens in all scenarios involving instrumental conditioning, in which the animal's behavior is the cause of an environmental event (for example, pressing down a lever causes the occurrence of food or the termination of footshock).

Causal learning can be seen as a specialized and efficient mental tool that allows an animal to maximize the quality of its interaction with the environment; to reap the benefits while avoiding the dangers and, consequently, to maximize its chances in the competition for survival and reproduction. The kind of causal learning that is required to accomplish this is known as *causal detection*, or the ability to identify the different causal relations in the environment, adapting behavior accordingly. Causal detection can be achieved with virtually no need to appeal to higher-order cognitive processes. In fact, associative theories proposed for Pavlovian and instrumental conditioning are known precisely for being able to account for causal detection by appealing to low-level, automatic mechanisms that require minimal cognitive processing and, certainly, no conscious thinking[28].

But the studies on causal learning that I have discussed in this book (see Chapter 4) showed that animals, and specifically the rat, go well beyond causal detection: they also seem capable of *causal reasoning*. Drawing causal inferences is not a mere philosophical "time killer". As with simple causal detection, causal reasoning can be instrumental in order to better adjust one's behavior to the demands of the environment and, when possible, adjust the

---

[28] See, for example, Rescorla and Wagner (1972).

environment to oneself, further maximizing appetitive events (for example, food, water, or sexual partners) and reducing aversive events (for example, loss of rewards, or injury). Imagine the following scenario. An animal seeking food happens to encounter a series of fresh tracks (for example, smells, footprints, broken branches) that are normally left by a carnivorous animal of a larger size. In this simple case, this animal's behavior will normally turn on the "defensive mode", being alert in order to avoid becoming lunch. But let us make this scenario a bit more interesting. Let us now imagine that this animal is a scavenger that naturally feeds on the carrion left behind by carnivorous animals. In that case, the tracks are not only a signal of danger, but also a signal of food. Because the large predator is both a cause of its tracks and the carcasses it leaves behind, the presence of tracks indicates that the predator was recently present in the area and, thus, that a carcass (food, in this case) might be available nearby. Effective causal reasoning, then, means more chances to get food, something with unquestionable adaptive value.

Moreover, because behaviors well adjusted to the causal structure of the environment will tend to be free from redundant and spurious efforts, this learning will also provide the animal with some extra time; and, time, in the animal kingdom is an asset, akin to having an edge in competition. For example, consider two individuals, A and B, from the same species, both of them with the skills necessary to obtain the amount of food and water needed for their survival (causal detection). But imagine that, while individual A is merely adjusting its behavior to raw information (the perceived causal relations), individual B is capable of further processing this information (causal reasoning). As a consequence, individual B might be much more efficient than animal A in basic food-search skills. It might complete the search in less time, or it might be able to shorten the time between meals. In any case, it will have more free time, which can be devoted to the other interesting things in life, such as courting the other sex or rearing offspring.

The previous examples are not totally arbitrary. In fact, they parallel one of the studies[29] that I discussed in Chapter 4, a study that provided good evidence of causal reasoning in the rat. As you might remember, in those experiments the animals were first given light-tone pairings interspersed with light-food pairings. The causal structure was thus simple: the light separately produced two effects, tone and food. What did the rats learn? To begin with, when they were given the tone alone, they sought the food. This is something that does not necessarily require any causal reasoning. For example, had they simply learned that tone and food co-occurred (true, but not the whole truth) or that the tone causes the food (false), they would have achieved the same feat. Fortunately, this experiment went further. Some rats had the opportunity to cause the occurrence of the tone with their own behavior by pressing a lever. Interestingly, when their own behavior caused the occurrence of the tone, they did not check whether food had been delivered. This means that they had learned that, although the tone and food were co-occurring events, the tone did not cause the food. Rather, they were both caused by a light. On those trials on which the tone was presented alone, without being preceded by their response, they did check for food, presumably because they "assumed" that the light had been presented (although somehow missed) and this, in turn, meant that food should have been delivered as well. However, on those trials on which the tone followed their own behavior, there was no need to check for food. They had caused the tone, which meant that the light had not been presented and, hence, that food was not ready yet.

Think about what the results of this study imply. These animals are placed in a tiny device, a Skinner box, where distances are short and, thus, the food hopper cannot be too far away[30]. Also,

---

[29] See Blaisdell and cols. (2006), and Leising and cols. (2008).

[30] As a reference, the internal dimensions of the standard chamber of Med Associates
(Footnote continued on next page)

their schedule is not precisely busy. Contrary to a wild animal, these rats have no worries other than getting their meal in that little box in which they are placed by the experimenters. No danger, no predators, no prospect of females, and no babies to feed, only them and the hope for a meal in the Skinner box. And yet, they can choose not to check for food because, based on what they infer, it will not be available. An animal's need to maximize resources, specifically time and energy, is that strong.

WHEN NONSENSE MAKES SENSE

So far, I have discussed causal detection and causal reasoning as complementary processes, with causal reasoning taking on the information gathered by causal detection processes, and further elaborating on it. This view implicitly assumes that no contradiction takes place between the outcomes of causal detection and causal reasoning processes, that causal reasoning is just one more step beyond causal detection. As strange as it might sound, such contradiction is possible, and the outcomes of causal reasoning might sometimes disagree with and correct the outcomes of causal detection.

The above statement might not make much sense if we think of the products of causal detection processes as highly accurate representations of reality. If all that is to be corrected is an occasional mistake, why establish another layer of information processing to monitor and correct an odd error? Unfortunately, such an additional layer is very much needed, for causal detection processes not only fail regularly, but also systematically. Skinner's *superstitious behavior* study[31] provides a classic and much celebrated

---

(ENV-008) are 12 x 9.5 x 8.25 inches or 30.5 x 24.1 x 21 cm (L x W x H). (Information retrieved on 01/27/2010 from http://tinyurl.com/yzkqh25.)

[31] Skinner (1948a).

example of a systematic error in causal detection. In this study, pigeons were given food on a regular basis (every 15 seconds). This food was provided "for free", meaning that the animals were not required to make any operant response (for example, pecking on an illuminated key) in order to get it. Nevertheless, the animals somehow connected idiosyncratic responses with the delivery of food, resulting in the strengthening of these responses throughout the experiment. In Skinner's words:

> *One bird was conditioned to turn counter-clockwise about the cage, making two or three turns between reinforcements. Another repeatedly thrust its head into one of the upper corners of the cage. A third developed a 'tossing' response, as if placing its head beneath an invisible bar and lifting it repeatedly. Two birds developed a pendulum motion of the head and body, in which the head was extended forward and swung from right to left with a sharp movement followed by a somewhat slower return. The body generally followed the movement and a few steps might be taken when it was extensive. Another bird was conditioned to make incomplete pecking or brushing movements directed toward but not touching the floor.*[32]

As much as we would like to believe so, pigeons are not the only animals who suffer from the irrationality of superstitions. Similar evidence has been found in rats[33] and, sadly enough, in humans too[34]. But, why is such a blatant mistake so popular in the animal kingdom? In other words, what makes our causality detection kit so vulnerable to this error? The answer, once again, can be found in our shared evolutionary history. Only when we think of the two possible ways in which a causality detection process could fail and of the differential impact of the

---

[32] Ibid, p. 168.

[33] Davis and Hubbard (1973).

[34] See, for example, Buskist, Miller, and Bennett (1980); Catania and Cutts (1963); Ono (1987); and Weisberg and Kennedy (1969).

consequences of each failure on the survival rate of the organism, we can understand that superstitious behaviors are the "lesser of two evils".

These two "evils" are nothing but the two legendary statistical error types: the Type I error (or α error, or *false positive*) and its "nemesis", the Type II error (or β error, or *false negative*). In statistics, these errors regard the probability of mistakenly accepting or rejecting the so-called *null hypothesis* or, simply put, the hypothesis that there is no significant difference between two or more samples or groups. Specifically, an α error is made when we reject the null hypothesis, and this hypothesis is actually correct. In other words, this error consists of stating that there is a difference between the samples when, in fact, there is none. Conversely, a β error is made when we accept the null hypothesis, and this hypothesis is actually false. That is, this error consists of stating that there is no difference between the samples when they do actually differ. By convention, scientists agree that the α error must be smaller than 0.05, or 5%, which renders the β error in at least 0.95, or 95%[35]. In other words, the statistical criteria used by scientists in their research leave little room for false positives, and wide room for false negatives. This is the same as to say that scientists choose rigor and accuracy over the laxity of guesses, even when much time and effort will be invested in failed experiments (a statistical significance of, say, 0.051 or, for that sake, 0.05001, is not acceptable, no matter how close it might be to meeting the criterion).

On any given day, relatively complex animals must make multiple choices. These choices could be right, thereby yielding profit (for example, food, sex, warmth, protection) or wrong,

---

[35] Requiring an α error smaller than 0.05 for statistical significance is typical in the social sciences, such as psychology. Natural sciences are more demanding, and have adopted a more stern standard, with an α error smaller than 0.01.

thereby yielding cost (for example, pain, illness, discomfort, loss of previously earned profits, and even death). Interestingly, animal behavior can fail to be adaptive in two radically different ways: by taking place when it was not necessary, and by not taking place when it was necessary. For example, an animal might smell or hear something that reminds it of a predator and, accordingly, make a defensive response (for example, freezing, fleeing, or hiding). Whether this response was correct or not depends on whether there really was a predator nearby. If there was a predator, this response was adaptive (a literal life-saver) but, if there was no predator, it can be said that this animal erroneously made a defensive response. In the statistical jargon of the previous paragraph, we could say that this animal just made an α error. For the sake of convenience, we will refer to this kind of error in regards to animal behavior merely as a *false positive* (in this case, we could also call this error a *false alarm*). This false positive carries a cost to the animal, ranging from a loss of energy and time to losing imminent access to rewards, such as food or sexual partners (activities that might have been interrupted by the putative predator). In an extreme case, in which false positives like this happen too often, the animal's survival might even be at stake (think of how, in humans, chronic fear can hinder one's life by eliciting defensive behaviors in situations that pose no real threat).

There is, of course, an alternative scenario. Let us assume that this animal detected the smell or noise, but failed to infer the presence of a predator, therefore failing to display the appropriate defensive behavior. Of course, it could be that no predator was really around, in which case the only adaptive defensive behavior would be the one that never happened. But, what if the predator was really nearby? In this case, failure to make a defensive behavior could be really costly, if not fatal. This latter error is, in statistical jargon, a β error. We will refer to this error as a *false negative*. In this example, it is easy to see that a false positive and a false negative do not necessarily carry the same potential penalty to the animal. The cost of a false positive is relatively low (wasted energy, time, and opportunity), whereas the cost of a false negative can be too high (injury or death).

In case you were wondering, this is not a conclusion that applies exclusively to (nonhuman) animals, or to predator detection scenarios. Nature's tendency to harshly punish false negatives over false positives seems to be pervasive. Let us consider yet another example, this one having to do with causality detection (the topic of this section) in humans. Imagine that, after you eat a large portion of a delicious blueberry cake, you feel sick to your stomach. Before jumping to conclusions about the "obvious" role of the blueberry cake in your misery, consider the following. Here we have two events, which might be causally related, or might not. Your stomach ache could be a consequence of food poisoning, and the blueberry cake could perfectly be guilty of your pain. But it could be something else, maybe a virus (for example, "stomach flu", *aka* gastroenteritis), or maybe excess of stimulants (for example, nicotine, or caffeine). So, you have two choices. On one hand, you could learn and remember these two events, cake and illness, as causally related, with cake being the cause and illness the effect. On the other hand, you could learn them as causally unrelated from each other (their contiguous occurrence was a mere coincidence). In any case, you can be right or you can be wrong. Say that you detect a causal connection between cake and illness and, as a consequence, you avoid eating this cake in the future. If got it right, you will no longer be exposed to a dangerous and, possibly, even life-threatening food. If, by contrast, you got it wrong then you will just miss some tasty food and, unless you are starving, this should be no big deal. Now, what if you detected no causal connection between cake and illness? In this case, if you got it right, then you are likely to make room for more cake in your fridge (and in your adipose tissue). But, if you got it all wrong, you might be in for an emergency visit to the nearest hospital.

It is clear from the previous examples that the price tag of a false positive is negligible compared to that of a false negative. Thus, in both the "predator detection" and the "blueberry cake" examples, the choice that might result in a possible false positive is preferred over the choice that might yield a false negative. This means that it is a better option to detect a predator (even when there might be none) and to attribute a causal role of blueberry cakes regarding illness (even when they can be harmless), than failing to do so. In other words, nature promotes a "better safe than sorry" policy among organisms, which can be said to translate in ultrasensitive detection systems: those animals with very low thresholds in their detection systems will more likely survive and reproduce, thereby passing on their ultrasensitive detection systems to their offspring. (Needless to say, some degree of discrimination is still necessary, for a system yielding continuous false alarms will be just as useless as a system yielding none.) Just like hypersensitive security or fire alarms might save more lives than less "picky" alarms (admittedly, with the inconvenience of occasional scares and headaches), psychological mechanisms that are likely to overreact to environmental events will more likely guarantee the survival of the organism in which it resides. After all, these psychological mechanisms form part of minds built by genes whose agenda includes one single goal, a goal that necessarily requires of the organism's survival – the genes' own replication.

And so, after this long digression, we can now see that superstitious behavior is no more than the result of a faulty causality detection process that has been long-favored in our evolutionary history. Because natural selection will strongly punish those individuals who make omission errors (false negatives) over those who make commission errors (false positives), it will support causality detection mechanisms that make causal connections almost by default, provided minimal conditions, such as the contiguous co-occurrence of the events. The behavior of those pigeons in Skinner's superstition experiment might seem amusing to us, who happen to know that food was provided for free or, in other words, that the actual contingency between their behavior and food was zero. However, from a hungry animal's perspective, that waste of energy was not too bad, especially compared to the alternative possibility: missing a meal for not having made a silly counter-clockwise or tossing move.

OVERCOMING SUPERSTITIONS

Given the apparent preference of natural selection for false negatives under uncertain conditions, it might seem like we (humans and nonhuman animals alike) are doomed to superstition. However, overcoming superstition can actually be easy. Human learning experiments on *illusion of control*[36] (the cognitive side of superstitious behavior, or the detection of a causal link between our behavior and environmental consequences when there is none) showed that college students exposed to a zero-contingency scenario developed the usual illusion of control when the instructions merely encouraged them to obtain the outcome (naturalistic condition), but accurately detected a null contingency when the instructions encouraged them to find out to what extent their behavior allowed them to control the outcome (analytic condition). The effect of the instructions on the participants' causal judgments seemed to be related to the probability of responding in each condition. In the naturalistic condition, the participants responded at a very high rate (on almost all trials), while in the analytic condition the participants responded much less (approximately on half of the trials). As a consequence of this differential rate of responding, the students in the naturalistic condition never had a chance to ascertain whether the outcome could also occur without their response. By contrast, those students in the analytic condition realized that the outcome occurred without

---

[36] Matute (1996).

their response as well and, thus, inferred that their response was not necessary to produce the outcome after all.

Like Skinner's original superstition study with pigeons[37], most experiments that examine superstitious behavior in nonhuman animals involve a naturalistic setting, in which hungry or thirsty animals are usually exposed to a zero-contingency situation involving their behavior and an outcome consisting of the food or water they are deprived of. As I said before, these animals cannot afford the luxury of behaving in an analytic manner to determine if their behavior really affects the probability of the outcome – for these animals, an analytic approach could imply losing their meal. As a consequence, these animals will normally respond at a high rate. Thus, the occurrence of the food/water reinforcer will be often preceded by their behavior and, therefore, they will likely draw a (non-existing) causal connection between their response and the reinforcer.

In truth, hungry/thirsty animals have very good reasons to be superstitious. So do most animals in the wild, for which stepping back to accurately determine the real contingency could prove deadly. Natural selection has operated upon thousands of generations of individuals that lived under very harsh circumstances, for which a life free of superstitious behavior (and illusion of control) was simply not an option. And, remember, natural selection does not "care" about anything but survival rate and reproductive fitness. An organism that lives long enough to reproduce, as superstitious as its behavior might be, is a winner in the struggle for life. This means that even those animals that could afford to adopt an analytic approach (responding less frequently in order to ascertain whether the response is, in fact, causally connected to environmental events) will not have the inclination to

---

[37] Skinner (1948a).

do so, if only because it is not the default approach in their innate repertoire. A satiated (non-deprived) rat might draw the same false connections between its response and the delivery of food/water as a hungry/thirsty rat. We, humans, are no exception. Many of us now live comfortable lives with plenty of free time on our hands and, yet, we enthusiastically devote ourselves to superstitions of all kinds, from carrying with us good luck charms, amulets, or talismans, to performing the rituals that religions establish as standard methods of communication with a deity.

This is not to say that our superstitions cannot be overcome. Adopting an analytic approach was enough in the aforementioned human contingency learning study[38] to completely eliminate illusion of control. All it takes is to behave like an intuitive scientist, systematically manipulating our own behavior and assessing its environmental impact, in order to accurately determine whether a real causal role can be attributed to our actions. Natural selection might have endowed us with a mind that is prone to the fallacy of superstitions and illusions, but this is a mind that has the potential to overcome its own innate tendencies. We might be born with a superstitious mindset, but we can learn to leave it behind by making use of our reasoning skills and by employing analytic thinking, along with a dose of critical thinking and skepticism. Of course, this will require a little effort for, while superstitious thinking comes easy, critical thinking does not. Just as indulging in fatty and sugary food demands less effort than eating vegetables and other healthy foods, or watching TV demands less effort than studying for an exam, seeing illusory connections around us is easier than following a rational approach to understanding our world. Reason does not come free, but this is a price worth paying considering that the alternative is wasting our lives continuously turning counter-clockwise in our cages for nothing.

---

[38] Matute (1996).

THINKING IS OVERRATED

We have seen that, from an evolutionary standpoint, thinking is an adaptation like any other. From this viewpoint, thinking is useful to the extent that it improves survival and reproductive fitness but, other than that, there is nothing special about it. To a species that calls itself *Homo sapiens* this might seem offensive. However, it is important to put things in perspective, even if our feelings get a little damaged in the process. Human intelligence is a product of evolution, it evolved through our ancestors' struggle to solve the problems of their daily lives, usually problems related to survival and mating. Human (and nonhuman) intelligence is not the only possible solution, but just one option among many. Evolving stronger and faster muscles, sharper teeth, or longer necks; producing poison to kill prey or to avoid becoming prey; blending with the background (camouflage) or imitating other animals (mimicry)... all those, and many more, are perfectly good alternatives as well.

Like anything in life, high intelligence comes with a cost: it requires a large brain. Across species, brain size positively correlates with intelligence. It is no surprise, thus, that *Homo sapiens* is the brainiest species, since human evolution has mostly consisted of increasingly larger cranial volumes. Of course, we are paying the price for having such huge brains, from birth complications (the mother's birth canal is not wide enough) and possible injuries (a consequence of having such large heads), to basic maintenance (the human brain represents 2% of our body weight, but consumes 20% the energy and nutrients required by the body).

Obviously, in the case of humans the benefits of such large brain (intelligence) exceed the costs. If this was not the case, our intelligence (and brains) would have not evolved. There is no reason why any species for which the costs of intelligence (large brains) outweighed the benefits should evolve into a more intelligent form. After all, a human-like intelligence is of no use to a species whose lifestyle does not pose human-like challenges, for these are the challenges that promoted the evolution of our intelligence in the past. Again, take the example of the rat. A rat's intelligence is obviously less sophisticated than ours and, yet, this animal thrives all around the world. It is its limited intelligence combined with other powerful traits (for example, high fertility, immune system, and omnivorous diet) that endow this animal with its extraordinary fitness.

OUR INNER RAT

In his book *The Ancestor's Tale*[39], Richard Dawkins takes the reader to a trip back in time through the evolutionary history of our species, telling the story of our most recent *common ancestors* (or *concestor*, as he calls them) with other living species. Travel back 6 million years, and the story of our *rendezvous point* with chimpanzees and bonobos is told; 7 million years marks our next *rendezvous point*, this time with gorillas; 14 to 18 million years, and we meet our concestors with orangutans and gibbons, respectively. After this point, we leave our ape relatives, and meet our monkey concestors, first with Old Word monkeys (25 million years) and then with New World monkeys (40 million years). Prosimian primates come next in this travel back in time and, only a few million years earlier, we arrive at our *rendezvous point* with rodents, a concestor that lived around 75 million years ago. That is, 75 million years ago, a species existed that evolved into other species, which in turn separately evolved into other species, among them humans and rats[40].

---

[39] Dawkins (2004).

[40] It would be a mistake to assume that this concestor resembled the rat or, for the sake, any currently living rodent species. The view of human evolution as a series of splits with currently living species is nothing but wrong, although sadly widespread. This is especially true in relation to our closest relative, the chimpanzee. We did not split from chimpanzees, as some claim (perhaps misinformed, perhaps ill-intentioned). Rather, we shared a

(Footnote continued on next page)

Based on the evidence discussed in this book, what can we tell about our concestor with the rat? Most likely, this animal was already capable of thinking similarly to our laboratory rat. That is, this animal was likely able to (among other things) detect causal relations and reason about them, it was also able to think about its own knowledge (metacognition), had an episodic-like memory that allowed it to mentally travel in time, could engage in generalized and direct reciprocity and, every now and then, would sigh in relief and laugh when tickled by a peer. The reason why this extinct animal can be presumed to do all this is not just because the laboratory rat can do it, but because we can do it too. That is, these mental traits can be posited to be (evolutionarily) homologous to rats and humans. This is no more, no less, than a straightforward application of Occam's razor (the principle of parsimony): given that two or more descendants of the same ancestor share this list of mental traits, we can either assume that they were already present in the common ancestor and were then passed on to their descendants (they are *homologous* or *primitive characters*) or, alternatively, assume that they were not present in the common ancestor and then evolved independently in the descendants (they are *analogous characters*, product of *convergent evolution*). Because of our shared ancestry with the rat, Occam's razor dictates that homology should be preferred over analogy[41]. Of course, accepting that these mental

---

concestor with chimpanzees. This concestor does no longer exist in its original form; it is actually extinct. However, this extinct concestor evolved into the species we know as chimpanzees (and bonobos), as well as humans. This also means that, not only humans have evolved ever since we shared our concestor with the chimpanzee, the chimpanzee has evolved too.

The idea that humans continue evolving, while leaving other species behind, stuck in an "evolutionary ladder" might be yet another attempt of (some) humans to preserve the pride of *Homo sapiens*. After all, seen this way it looks like evolution happened with one single goal: creating and, then, improving us. Admitting that we are not the end product (nor a perfect one) of natural selection is just the first step towards understanding evolution.

[41] A classical example of analogy or convergent evolution regards the wing, which has independently evolved in insects, birds, and bats. Analogy does not exclusively relate to

(Footnote continued on next page)

processes are homologous to rats and humans necessarily implies that they should also appear in *all other descendants* of our common ancestor with the rat. This seems to be the case. Thus far, nonhuman primates have been found to be capable of all this, and much more[42].

In sum, the comparative study of animal cognition allows us to figuratively travel back in time and ascertain the mentality of our own ancestors. It has been around 75 million years since we split from the rat in our evolutionary journey and, yet, we share some of the most important building blocks of our mentality with this tiny animal. Like it or not, we all carry an inner rat.

---

physical traits, but to mental and/or behavioral traits as well (see Emery & Clayton, 2004, for a discussion on the convergent evolution of mental traits in corvids and apes).

[42] There are excellent books devoted to primate cognition, which cover the topics discussed in the present book in regards to rat cognition. See, for example, Byrne (1995) and Tomasello and Call (1997). This is, however, a very active research field and the literature grows fast. The interested reader is advised to search the scientific journals for recent research.

APPENDIX A: WHAT'S AHEAD?

This book has told the story of the rat as an experimental subject in psychological research, both in the traditional field of animal learning and in the more recently developed field of animal cognition. By means of telling the story of this laboratory animal, this book has also covered (at least partially) the historical transition of scientific ideas, from the original radical behaviorist framework to the cognitive orientation that permeates current research. To be fair, this book is as much about the rat as it is about the men and women who have studied this animal in their laboratories over the past decades.

But the experiments described in this book are still rather exceptional in the field, and have been produced by a very short list of research teams scattered across the United States and Europe. One might wonder if this kind of research is just a historical oddity, another ephemeral fashion or, to the contrary, the first baby steps toward a new research area. Of course, it is a matter of guessing at this point, but it all seems to indicate that we are witnessing the launch of a brand new line of research in animal psychology.

To make sure that this impression is not merely the product of wishful thinking on my part, I decided to do some armchair research. Using one of the standard databases of psychological publications (PsycINFO®), I searched for the number of publications over the last century containing specific keywords. The first search used the keywords *animal* and *cognition*. As can be appreciated in the following graph, this search yielded virtually no entries from 1901 to 1990. However, this flat line takes off during the decade of 1991-2000, when more than 1,000 publications are found. Moreover, during the decade of 2001-2010 the number tripled (and note that this number did not include all the publications of 2010). Nevertheless, these numbers might underestimate the actual number of publications on this topic, as shown by the large amount of entries under the keywords *comparative* and *psychology*: around 10,000 publications in the last decade, slightly better than during the productive years of 1961-1980, and recovering from the (mysterious) steep decline of the 1980s. By contrast, it is clear that the use of the word *animal* along with *intelligence* still remains unpopular in the literature. The number of publications containing these words is still negligible (around 500 publications in the last decade – and this is the largest number in more than 100 years).

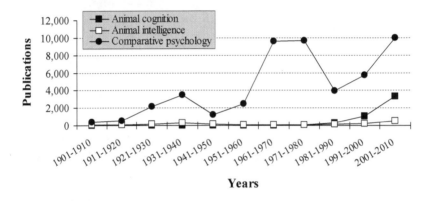

Number of publications found under the keywords *animal+cognition*, *animal+intelligence*, and *comparative+psychology* from 1901 to 2010, as found using PsycINFO® (search performed on 05/27/2010).

A comparable inspection of the number of publications also brings good news to the field of animal learning, as shown by the next graph. Interestingly, while the number of publications found with the keywords *animal* and *learning* has grown steadily since 1990, the number of publications under *animal* and *conditioning* seemingly hit a ceiling below 4,000 publications per decade after 1960. This observation is interesting on its own, since it indicates a preference for the more inclusive term "learning" (which is open to a cognitive orientation) than the term "conditioning" (with a distinct behaviorist flavor). In addition, it is worth pointing out that the increasing number of animal learning publications over the last two decades seemingly overlaps in time with the rise of interest in animal cognition and comparative psychology. This might be mere coincidence, of course, but it would not be surprising to find that common reasons underlie the strengthening of these related fields of research.

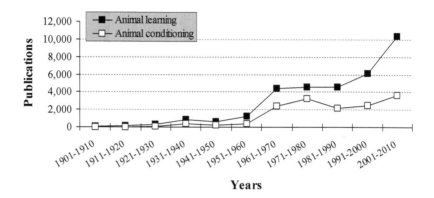

Number of publications found under the keywords *animal+learning* and *animal+conditioning* from 1901 to 2010, as found using PsycINFO® (search performed on 05/27/2010).

Even when, as evidenced by the previous two graphs, the scientific study of the mentality of animals is still alive, it is no secret to anyone that, right now, the real "gold rush" is happening not in the study of the mind, but in the study of the organ that makes the mind possible. This is obvious in the third and final graph, which depicts the number of publications found on one hand under the keywords *biological* and *psychology* (*aka biopsychology*) and, on the other hand, under the keywords *behavioral* and *neuroscience* (the current term for biopsychology) Although both terms have gained popularity over the last two decades, they have undergone a tremendous increase in visibility over the last decade. This is especially true for behavioral neuroscience, which almost tripled in number of publications from 1991-2000 to 2001-2010 (and note the larger scale in the y-axis in this last graph – here "tripled" actually means an increase from almost 6,000 publications to more than 19,000.)

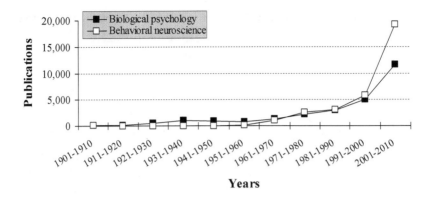

Number of publications found under the keywords *biological+psychology* and *behavioral+neuroscience* from 1901 to 2010, as found using PsycINFO® (search performed on 05/27/2010).

The bottom line is that, no matter where exactly one decides to focus his or her research (brain, mind, or behavior); there is a bright future ahead for experimental psychology involving nonhuman animals. And it seems that the albino rat will continue to support the quest for knowledge of our generation, and in the generations to come. Along the way, it might also provide our researchers with a few more provocative findings. Who knows, perhaps in a few years the claims in this book will be obsolete, but generally accepted. Perhaps, in a few years, the behaviorist view of the rat as a mechanical stimulus-response organism will be an old fashioned idea, dismissed as simplistic in light of the large and growing amount of evidence proving, to the contrary, that rats do think. And, along with this realization, perhaps we, humans, might step down from our imaginary throne in the animal kingdom. Only once we leave behind our anthropocentric ideal of intelligence, will we be able to admire the richness of other animals' mental life. In doing so, we might actually end up respecting and protecting our nonhuman relatives.

Now, this is a good cause.

APPENDIX B: WHAT'S LEFT FOR OUR EGO?

This book has discussed evidence of a series of mental abilities in nonhuman animals (with special emphasis on the rat), which have been traditionally considered exclusive feats of *Homo sapiens*. The authors of these studies, far from avoiding the philosophical implications of their findings, explicitly take on this issue. Take, for example, the abilities discussed in Chapter 4, namely, causal reasoning and metacognition. For instance, Beckers and his collaborators mentioned that their findings "[endow] relatively simple mammals such as rats with remarkable cognitive abilities, rather than confining these capabilities to higher mammals such as humans and (some) other apes."[1] Similarly, Blaisdell and his collaborators stated that "[a] number of researchers have recently concluded that causal reasoning is a faculty that divides humans from animals [...]. The present results cast doubt on that conclusion."[2], and that their demonstration of causal reasoning in rats "weaken[s] the argument that there is a sharp dividing line with respect to causal reasoning between human and nonhuman animals"[3]. In the very first line of their report, Foote and Crystal state that "[the] ability to reflect on one's own mental processes, termed metacognition, is a defining feature of human existence"[4]. In a report titled *Metacognition in the rat*, such opening sentence should leave no doubt regarding the direction the authors are taking.

Animal cognition researchers are, thus, perfectly aware of the

---

[1] Beckers and cols. (2006), p. 100.

[2] Blaisdell and cols. (2006), p. 1022.

[3] Leising and cols. (2008), p. 526.

[4] Foote and Crystal (2007), p. 551.

deep implications of their studies. They know that each of their experiments further chip away at the pedestal on which the human species has historically placed itself in relation to other species. The more research on animal cognition is conducted, it seems, the more the dividing lines separating us from the rest of the animals are blurred. Interestingly, the study of cognition in animals might eventually achieve what the study of behavior in its purest form could not: to unite human and nonhuman psychology in a common framework. Radical behaviorism tried this by "lowering" humans to the level of nonhuman animals (from this viewpoint, human and nonhuman behavior equally obeys simple mechanistic principles), and failed. Animal cognition is following the contrary approach, bringing nonhuman animals closer to the level of humans (from this perspective, both human and nonhuman behavior is the result of complex cognitive processes). The trick, it seems, was to get over the *mind taboo* of behaviorism and accept that nonhuman animals (and humans too) have a mind that can perfectly be the subject of scientific research.

Is there anything left for our ego? Not much, apparently. Most of the intellectual abilities traditionally considered benchmarks of human superiority are now long gone. Studies on primate cognition[5] have shown that nonhuman apes, are capable of "typically human" skills such as using and making tools, linguistic communication (for example, American sign language effectively used by chimpanzees and gorillas), self-recognition in the mirror, or the so called *theory of mind* (understanding that other individuals are entities with a mind, and that the contents of those minds might resemble, and also differ from, your own). Evidence of intelligence in nonhuman primates can be quite difficult to digest for those who rely on the presumption of belonging to a species that was, in the eyes of its presumed creator, a state-of-the-art product. But the list

---

[5] For a review, see Byrne (1995).

does not end there. There is now evidence of linguistic communication and rich cognitive skills in the African Grey Parrot[6], and of tool using and tool making in the crow[7], let alone evidence of primate-like intelligence in dolphins and elephants[8]. To make things worse (for those whose ego squirms in light of this evidence, that is), experiments like the ones discussed in this book indicate that the rat seems to have the cognitive rudiments of psychological processes (like metacognition, see Chapter 4) that even philosophers only granted to the human being[9].

Thus, the question of what is left that humans (and only humans) are exclusive at is a tricky one. One could elaborate a relatively short list today, but knowing that the list would be even shorter tomorrow makes this task pointless. The differences, it seems, are quantitative rather than qualitative[10]. Our underlying processes seem to be pretty much the same, but our huge computational power allows us to reach levels of performance that nonhuman animals could not even dream of.

---

[6] See Pepperberg (2002), for a description of her studies with *Alex*, a truly amazing parrot.

[7] See Weir, Chappell, and Kacelnik (2002). In this research, the crow *Betty* seemed to be especially skillful in bending a wire to make her perfect food-retrieval hook. For photos and videos showing this evidence, visit the website of this research team at http://tinyurl.com/yg8cakm. Also, see Emery and Clayton (2004) for a review of this and other interesting studies.

[8] For example, there is recent evidence of mirror self-recognition in the bottlenose dolphin (Reiss & Marino, 2001) and an Asian elephant (Plotnik, De Waal, & Reiss, 2006).

[9] Neuroscience seems to be following the lead of psychology in regards to the recognition of the rat as an animal with a higher cognitive status (see Abbott, 2010).

[10] Of course, a philosopher might raise the hand now. We might not be the only species that thinks (cognition), nor the only species that reflects on our thoughts (metacognition), but we might be the only species with *metametacognition*, or the ability to think about thinking about our thoughts, which is what I did in the corresponding section of Chapter 4, when I discussed (and, in the process, thought) about metacognition. Do animals have the ability of recursivity *ad infinitum* that most humans (if not all, at least philosophers and mathematicians) have? If not, is this the ultimate proof of the intellectual superiority of our species?

For updates and further discussion, join our Facebook group at **http://tinyurl.com/TTR4FB**.

 For contact information and other resources, visit the author's website at **http://www.opineno.com**.

REFERENCES

Abbott, A. (2010). The rat pack. *Nature, 465,* 282-283.

Allan, L. G. (1980). A note on measurement of contingency between two binary variables in judgement tasks. *Bulletin of the Psychonomic Society, 15,* 147-149.

Annau, Z., & Kamin, L. J. (1961). The conditioned emotional response as a function of intensity of the US. *Journal of Comparative and Physiological Psychology, 54,* 428-432.

Axelrod, R., & Hamilton, W. D. (1981). The evolution of cooperation. *Science, 211,* 1390-1396.

Babb, S. J., & Crystal, J. D. (2005). Discrimination of what, when, and where: Implications for episodic-like memory in rats. *Learning and Motivation, 36,* 177-189.

Babb, S. J., & Crystal, J. D. (2006). Episodic-like memory in the rat. *Current Biology, 16,* 1317-1321.

Baker, A. G., Murphy, R. A., & Vallée-Tourangeau, F. (1996). Associative and normative models of causal induction: Reacting to versus understanding cause. In D. R. Shanks, K. J. Holyoak, & D. L. Medin (Eds.), *The psychology of learning and motivation, Vol. 34: Causal learning* (pp. 1-45). San Diego, CA: Academic Press.

Barnett, S. A. (2001). *The story of rats: Their impact on us, and our impact on them.* Crows Nest, Australia: Allen & Unwin.

Beckers, T., De Houwer, J., Pineño, O., & Miller, R. R. (2005). Outcome additivity and outcome maximality influence cue competition in human causal learning. *Journal of Experimental Psychology: Learning, Memory, and Cognition, 31,* 238-249.

Beckers, T., Miller, R. R., De Houwer, J., & Urushihara, K. (2006). Reasoning rats: Forward blocking in Pavlovian animal conditioning is sensitive to constraints of causal inference. *Journal of Experimental Psychology: General, 135,* 92-102.

Belliveau, J. W., Kennedy, D. N., McKinstry, R. C., Buchbinder, B. R., Weisskoff, R. M., Cohen, M. S., Vevea, J. M., Brady, T. J., & Rosen, B. R. (1991). Functional mapping of the human visual cortex by magnetic resonance imaging. *Science, 254,* 716-719.

Black, S. L.. (2003). Pavlov's dogs: For whom the bell rarely tolled. *Current Biology, 13,* R426.

Blaisdell, A. P., Leising, K. J., Stahlman, W. D., & Waldmann, M. R. (2009). Rats distinguish between absence of events and lack of information in sensory preconditioning. *International Journal of Comparative Psychology, 22,* 1-18.

Blaisdell, A. P., Sawa, K., Leising, K. J., & Waldmann, M. R. (2006). Causal reasoning in rats. *Science, 311,* 1020-1022.

Boakes, R. A. (1984). *From Darwin to behaviourism: Psychology and the minds of animals.* New York: Cambridge University Press.

Bouton, M. E. (2007). *Learning and behavior. A contemporary synthesis.* Sunderland, MA: Sinauer Associates.

Breland, K., & Breland, M. (1961). The misbehavior of organisms. *American Psychologist, 16,* 681-684.

Brodgen, W. J. (1939). Sensory preconditioning. *Journal of Experimental Psychology, 25,* 323-332.

Buskist, W. F., Miller, H. L., & Bennett, R. H. (1980). Fixed-interval performance in humans: Sensitivity to temporal parameters when food is the reinforcer. *Psychological Record, 30,* 111-121.

Byrne, R. (1995). *The thinking ape. Evolutionary origins of intelligence.* New York: Oxford University Press.

Calhoun, J. B. (1962). Population density and social pathology. *Scientific American, 206,* 139-148.

Carreiras, M., Lopez, J., Rivero, F., & Corina, D. (2005). Neural processing of a whistled language. *Nature, 433,* 31-32.

Catania, A. C., & Cutts, D. (1963). Experimental control of superstitious responding in humans. *Journal of the Experimental Analysis of Behavior, 6,* 203-208.

Church, R. M. (1959). Emotional reactions of rats to the pain of others. *Journal of Comparative and Physiological Psychology, 52,* 132-134.

Clayton, N. S., Bussey, T. J., & Dickinson, A. (2003). Can animals recall the past and plan for the future? *Nature Reviews Neuroscience, 4,* 685-691.

Clayton, N. S., & Dickinson, A. (1998). Episodic-like memory during cache recovery by scrub jays. *Nature, 395,* 272-274.

Clayton, N., & Dickinson, A. (2006). Rational rats. *Nature Neuroscience, 9,* 472-474.

Colwill, R. M., & Rescorla, R. A. (1986). Associative structures in instrumental learning. In G. H. Bower (Ed.), *The psychology of learning and motivation* (pp. 55-104). San Diego: Academic Press.

Coombes, S., Revusky, S., & Lett, B. T. (1980). Long-delay taste aversion learning in an unpoisoned rat: Exposure to a poisoned rat as the unconditioned stimulus. *Learning and Motivation, 11,* 256-266.

Darwin, C. (1859). *On the origin of species by means of natural selection, or the preservation of favoured races in the struggle for life.* London: John Murray.

Darwin, C. (1871). *The descent of man, and selection in relation to sex.* London: John Murray.

Darwin, C. (1872). *The expression of the emotions in man and animals.* London: John Murray.

Davis, H., & Hubbard, J. (1973). An analysis of superstitious behavior in the rat. *Behaviour, 43,* 1-12.

Dawkins, R. (1976). *The selfish gene.* New York: Oxford University Press.

Dawkins, R. (2004). *The ancestor's tale: A pilgrimage to the dawn of evolution.* New York: Mariner Books.

Dawkins, R. (2006). *The God delusion.* New York: Houghton Mifflin Company.

De Belle, J. S., & Heisenberg, M. (1994). Associative odor learning in *Drosophila* abolished by chemical ablation of mushroom bodies. *Science, 263,* 692-695.

De Houwer, J., & Beckers, T. (2002). A review of recent developments in research and theories on human contingency learning. *The Quarterly Journal of Experimental Psychology, 55B,* 289-310.

De Houwer, J., Beckers, T., & Glautier, S. (2002). Outcome and cue properties modulate blocking. *Quarterly Journal of Experimental Psychology: Human Experimental Psychology, 55A,* 965-985.

Denny, M. R. (1971). Relaxation theory and experiments. In F. R. Brush (Ed.), *Aversive conditioning and learning* (pp. 235-295). New York: Academic Press.

Descartes, R. (1637). *Discourse on method.* Cambridge, UK: Cambridge University Press.

Dickinson, A. (1980). *Contemporary animal learning theory.* Cambridge, UK: Cambridge University Press.

Dickinson, A., & Balleine, B. (1994). Motivational control of goal-directed action. *Animal Learning & Behavior, 22,* 1-18.

Dobzhansky, T. (1973). Nothing in biology makes sense except in the light of evolution. *American Biology Teacher, 35,* 125-129.

Domjan, M. (2009). *The principles of learning and behavior.* Belmont, CA: Wadsworth.

Dwyer, D. M., Starns, J., & Honey, R. C. (2009). "Causal reasoning" in rats: A reappraisal. *Journal of Experimental Psychology: Animal Behavior Processes, 35,* 578-586.

Emery, N. J., & Clayton, N. S. (2004). The mentality of crows: Convergent evolution of intelligence in corvids and apes. *Science, 306,* 1903-1907.

Foote, A. L., & Crystal, J. D. (2007). Metacognition in the rat. *Current Biology, 17,* 551-555.

Foree, D. D., & LoLordo, V. M. (1973). Attention in the pigeon: The differential effects of food-getting vs. shock avoidance procedures. *Journal of Comparative and Physiological Psychology, 85,* 551-558.

Galef, B. G. (1996). Social enhancement of food preferences in Norway rats: A brief review. In C. M. Heyes & B. G. Galef (Eds.), *Social learning in animals: The roots of culture* (pp. 49-64). San Diego, CA: Academic Press.

Galle, O. R., Gove, W. R., & McPherson, J. M. (1972). Population density and pathology: What are the relations for man? *Science, 176,* 23-30.

Garcia, J., & Koelling, R. A. (1966). Relation of cue to consequence in avoidance learning. *Psychonomic Science, 4,* 123-124.

Gill, T. J., Smith, G. J., Wissler, R. W., & Kunz, H. W. (1989). The rat as an experimental animal. *Science, 245,* 269-276.

Gleick, J. (1987). *Chaos: Making a new science.* New York: Penguin Books.

Greene, J., & Haidt, J. (2002). How (and where) does moral judgment work? *Trends in Cognitive Sciences, 6,* 517-523.

Haselgrove, M. (2010). Reasoning rats or associative animals? A common-element analysis of the effects of additive and subadditive pretraining on blocking. *Journal of Experimental Psychology: Animal Behavior Processes, 36,* 296-306.

Healy, S. D., & Hurly, T. A. (1995). Spatial memory in rufous hummingbirds (*Selasphorus rufus*): A field test. *Animal Learning & Behavior, 23,* 63-68.

Holland, P. C. (1981). Acquisition of representation-mediated conditioned food aversions. *Learning and Motivation, 12,* 1-18.

Holland, P. C., & Rescorla, R. A. (1975). The effect of two ways of devaluing the unconditioned stimulus after first- and second-order appetitive conditioning. *Journal of Experimental Psychology: Animal Behavior Processes, 1,* 355-363.

Hume, D. (1964). *Treatise of human nature* (L. A. Selby-Bigge, Ed.). London: Oxford University Press. (Original work published 1739).

Kamin, L. J. (1968). "Attention-like" processes in classical conditioning. In M. R. Jones (Ed.), *Miami symposium on the prediction of behavior: Aversive stimulation* (pp. 9-31). Miami, FL: University of Miami Press.

Kamin, L. J. (1969). Predictability, surprise, attention, and conditioning. In B. A. Campbell & M. R. Church (Eds.), *Punishment and aversive behavior* (pp. 279-296). New York: Appleton-Century-Crofts.

Killeen, P. R. (1978). Superstition: A matter of bias, not detectability. *Science, 199,* 88-90.

Knapp, T. J., & Robertson, L. C. (1986). *Approaches to cognition: Contrasts and controversies.* Hillsday, NJ: Lawrence Erlbaum Associates.

Korbo, L., Pakkenberg, B., Ladefoged, O., Gundersen, H. J., Arlien-Søborg, P., & Pakkenberg, H. (1990). An efficient method for estimating the total number of neurons in rat brain cortex. *Journal of Neuroscience Methods, 31,* 93-100.

Kuhn, T. S. (1962). *The structure of scientific revolutions.* Chicago, IL: The University of Chicago Press.

Lavin, M. J., Freise, B., & Coombes, S. (1980). Transferred flavor aversions in adult rats. *Behavioral and Neural Biology, 28,* 15-33.

Leahey, T. H. (2004). *A history of psychology: Main currents in psychological thought.* Upper Saddle River, NJ: Prentice-Hall.

Lee, A. K., & Wilson, M. A. (2002). Memory of sequential experience in the hippocampus during slow wave sleep. *Neuron, 36,* 1183-1194.

Leising, K. J., Wong, J., Waldmann, M. R., & Blaisdell, A. P. (2008). The special status of actions in causal reasoning in rats. *Journal of Experimental Psychology: General,* 137, 514-527.

Lemov, R. (2005). *World as laboratory: Experiments with mice, mazes, and men.* New York: Hill and Wang.

Lindsay, P. H., & Norman, D. A. (1972). *Human information processing. An introduction to psychology.* New York: Academic Press.

Livesey, E. J., & Boakes, R. A. (2004). Outcome additivity, elemental processing and blocking in human causality judgements. *Quarterly Journal of Experimental Psychology: Comparative and Physiological Psychology, 57B,* 361-379.

Louie, K., & Wilson, M. A. (2001). Temporally structured replay of awake hippocampal ensemble activity during rapid eye movement sleep. *Neuron, 29,* 145-156.

Lovibond, P. F., Been, S.-L., Mitchell, C. J., Bouton, M. E., & Frohardt, R. (2003). Forward and backward blocking of causal judgement is enhanced by additivity of effect magnitude. *Memory & Cognition, 31,* 133-142.

Markman, K. D., Klein, W. M. P., & Suhr, J. A. (2008). *Handbook of imagination and mental simulation.* New York: Psychology Press.

Matute, H. (1996). Illusion of control: Detecting response-outcome independence in analytic but not in naturalistic conditions. *Psychological Science, 7,* 289-293.

Miller, K. R. (2008). *Only a theory: Evolution and the battle for America's soul.* New York: Viking.

Miller, N. E. (1959). Liberalization of basic S-R concepts: Extensions to conflict behavior, motivational and social learning. In S. Koch (Ed.), *Psychology: A study of science, Vol. 2* (pp. 196-292). New York: McGraw-Hill.

Minsky, M. (1985). *The society of mind.* New York: Simon & Schuster.

Mitani, J. C., Watts, D. P., & Amsler, S. J. (2010). Lethal intergroup aggression leads to territorial expansion in wild chimpanzees. *Current Biology, 20,* R507-R508.

Mitchell, C. J., & Lovibond, P. F. (2002). Backward and forward blocking in human electrodermal conditioning: Blocking requires an assumption of outcome additivity. *Quarterly Journal of Experimental Psychology, 55B,* 311-329.

Nye, R. D. (1992). *The legacy of B. F. Skinner: Concepts and perspectives, controversies and misunderstandings.* Belmont, CA: Brooks/Cole.

Öhman, A., Dimberg, U., & Öst, L. G. (1985). Animal and social phobias: Biological constraints on learned fear responses. In S. Reiss & R. R. Bootzin (Eds.), *Theoretical issues in behavior therapy.* Orlando, FL: Academic Press.

Ono, K. (1987). Superstitious behavior in humans. *Journal of the Experimental Analysis of Behavior, 47,* 261-271.

Panksepp, J., & Burgdorf, J. (2003). "Laughing" rats and the evolutionary antecedents of human joy? *Physiology & Behavior, 79,* 533-547.

Pass, D., & Freeth, G. (1993). The rat. *ANZCCART News, 6,* 1-4.

Pavlov, I. P. (1927). *Conditioned reflexes.* London: Clarendon Press.

Pear, J. (2007). *A historical and contemporary look at psychological systems.* Mahwah, NJ: Lawrence Erlbaum Associates.

Penn, D. C., & Povinelli, D. J. (2007). Causal cognition in human and nonhuman animals: A comparative, critical review. *Annual Review of Psychology, 58,* 97-118.

Pepperberg, I. M. (2002). *The Alex studies: Cognitive and communicative abilities of Grey Parrots.* Cambridge, MA: Harvard University Press.

Piaget, J. (1954). *Construction of reality in the child.* New York: Norton. (Original work published 1937).

Pineño, O., & Miller, R. R. (2007). Comparing associative, statistical, and inferential reasoning accounts of human contingency learning. *The Quarterly Journal of Experimental Psychology, 60,* 310-329.

Pinker, S. (2009). *How the mind works.* New York: W. W. Norton & Company.

Plotnik, J. M., De Waal, F. B. M., & Reiss, D. (2006). Self-recognition in an Asian elephant. *PNAS, 103,* 17053-17057.

Polack, C. W., McConnell, B. L., & Miller, R. R. (2010). *Associative foundation of causal learning in rats (and humans?).* Manuscript submitted for publication.

Quinn, R. (2005). Comparing rat's to human's age: How old is my rat in people years? *Nutrition, 21,* 775-777.

Reiss, D., & Marino, L. (2001). Mirror self-recognition in the bottlenose dolphin: A case of cognitive convergence. *PNAS, 98,* 5937-5942.

Rescorla, R. A. (1968). Probability of shock in the presence and absence of CS in fear conditioning. *Journal of Comparative and Physiological Psychology, 66,* 1-5.

Rescorla, R. A., & Cunningham, C. L. (1978). Within-compound flavor associations. *Journal of Experimental Psychology: Animal Behavior Processes, 4,* 267-275.

Rescorla, R. A., & Freberg, L. (1978). The extinction of within-compound flavor associations. *Learning and Motivation, 9,* 411-427.

Rescorla, R. A., & Wagner, A. R. (1972). A theory of Pavlovian conditioning: Variations in the effectiveness of reinforcement and nonreinforcement. In A. H. Black & W. F. Prokasy (Eds.), *Classical conditioning II: Current research and theory* (pp. 64-99). New York: Appleton-Century-Crofts.

Richelle, M. N. (1993). *B. F. Skinner: A reappraisal.* East Sussex, UK: Psychology Press.

Rizley, R. C., & Rescorla, R. A. (1972). Associations in higher order conditioning and sensory preconditioning. *Journal of Comparative and Physiological Psychology, 81,* 1-11.

Romanes, G. J. (1882). *Animal intelligence.* New York: Appleton.

Ryle, G. (2002). *The concept of mind.* Chicago: University of Chicago Press. (Original work published 1949).

Rutte, C., & Taborsky, M. (2007). Generalized reciprocity in rats. *PLoS Biology, 5,* 1421-1425.

Rutte, C., & Taborsky, M. (2008). The influence of prior experience on cooperative behaviour in rats (Rattus norvegicus): Direct vs generalised reciprocity. *Behavioral Ecology and Sociobiology, 62,* 499-505.

Scott, E. C. (2005). *Evolution vs. creationism: An introduction.* Berkeley, CA. University of California Press.

Selfridge, O. G. (1959). Pandemonium: A paradigm for learning. In D. V. Blake & A. M. Uttley (Eds.), *Proceedings of the symposium on the mechanisation of thought processes* (pp. 511-529). London: HM Stationery Office.

Seligman, M. E. P. (1971). Phobias and preparedness. *Behavior Therapy, 2,* 307-320.

Seyfarth, R. M., Cheney, D. L., & Marler, P. (1980). Vervet monkey alarm calls: Semantic communication in a free-ranging primate. *Animal Behaviour, 28,* 1070-1094.

Shanks, D. R. (2007). Associationism and cognition: Human contingency learning at 25. *The Quarterly Journal of Experimental Psychology, 60,* 291-309.

Shanks, D. R., Lopez, F. J., Darby, R. J., & Dickinson, A. (1996). Distinguishing associative and probabilistic contrast theories of human contingency judgment. In D. R. Shanks, K. J. Holyoak, & D. L. Medin (Eds.), *The psychology of learning and motivation, Vol. 34: Causal learning* (pp. 265-311). San Diego, CA: Academic Press.

Shanks, D. R., Medin, D. L., & Holyoak, K. J. (1996). *The psychology of learning and motivation, Vol. 34: Causal learning.* San Diego, CA: Academic Press.

Shermer, M. (2006). *Why Darwin matters: The case against intelligent design.* New York: Holt.

Skinner, B. F. (1938). *The behavior of organisms: An experimental analysis.* New York: Appleton-Century.

Skinner, B. F. (1948a). 'Superstition' in the pigeon. *Journal of Experimental Psychology, 38,* 168-172.

Skinner, B. F. (1948b). *Walden Two.* New York: Macmillan.

Skinner, B. F. (1971). *Beyond freedom and dignity.* New York: Knopf.

Skinner, B. F. (1987). Whatever happened to psychology as the science of behavior? *American Psychologist, 42,* 780-786.

Skinner, B. F. (1990). Can psychology be a science of mind? *American Psychologist, 45,* 1206-1210.

Sloman, S. A., & Lagnado, D. A. (2005). Do we "do"? *Cognitive Science, 29,* 5-39.

Small, W. S. (1901). Experimental study of the mental processes of the rat. II. *The American Journal of Psychology, 12,* 206-239.

Soltysik, S., & Jelen, P. (2005). In rats, sighs correlate with relief. *Physiology & Behavior, 85,* 598-602.

Staddon, J. E. R., Jozefowiez, J., & Cerutti, D. (2007). Metacognition: A problem not a process. *PsyCrit, 1,* 1-5.

Stewart, C. C. (1898). Variations in daily activity produced by alcohol and by changes in barometric pressure and diet, with a description of recording methods. *American Journal of Physiology, 1,* 40-56.

Suckow, M. A., Weisbroth, S. H., & Franklin, C. L. (2006). *The laboratory rat.* Burlington, MA: Academic Press.

Sullivan, R. (2004). *Rats: Observations on the history and habitat of the City's most unwanted inhabitants.* New York: Bloomsbury.

Thorndike, E. L. (1911). *Animal intelligence: Experimental studies.* New York: Macmillan.

Timberlake, W., & Grant, D. L. (1975). Autoshaping in rats to the presentation of another rat predicting food. *Science, 190,* 690-692.

Tolman, E. C. (1932). *Purposive behavior in animals and men.* New York: The Century Co.

Tolman, E. C. (1938). The determiners of behavior at a choice point. *Psychological Review, 45,* 1-41.

Tolman, E. C. (1948). Cognitive maps in rats and men. *Psychological Review, 55*, 189-208.

Tolman, E. C., & Honzik, C. H. (1930). Introduction and removal of reward, and maze performance in rats. *University of California Publications in Psychology, 4*, 257-275.

Tomasello, M., & Call, J. (1997). *Primate cognition.* New York: Oxford University Press.

Trivers, R. L. (1971). The evolution of reciprocal altruism. *The Quarterly Review of Biology, 46*, 35-57.

Tully, T. (2003). Pavlov's dogs. *Current Biology, 13*, R117-R119.

Viana, D. S., Gordo, I., Sucena, E., & Moita, M. A. P. (2010). Cognitive and motivational requirements for the emergence of cooperation in a rat social game. *PLoS ONE, 5*, e8483.

Waldmann, M. R., & Hagmayer, Y. (2005). Seeing versus doing: Two modes of accessing causal knowledge. *Journal of Experimental Psychology: Learning, Memory, & Cognition, 31*, 216-227.

Wasserman, E. A., Franklin. S. R., & Hearst, E. (1974). Pavlovian appetitive contingencies and approach versus withdrawal to conditioned stimuli in pigeons. *Journal of Comparative and Physiological Psychology, 86*, 616-627.

Wasserman, E. A., Kao, S.-F., Van Hamme, L. J., Katagiri, M., & Young, M. E. (1996). Causation and association. In D. R. Shanks, K. J. Holyoak, & D. L. Medin (Eds.), *The psychology of learning and motivation, Vol. 34: Causal learning* (pp. 207-264). San Diego, CA: Academic Press.

Watson, J. B. (1913). Psychology as the behaviorist views it. *Psychological Review, 20*, 158-177.

Watson, J. B. (1997). *Behaviorism.* New Brunswick, NJ: Transaction Publishers. (Original work published 1924).

Watson, J. B., & Rayner, R. (1920). Conditioned emotional reactions. *Journal of Experimental Psychology, 3*, 1-14.

Weir, A. A. S., Chappell, J., & Kacelnik, A. (2002). Shaping of hooks in New Caledonian Crows. *Science, 297*, 981.

Weisberg, P., & Kennedy, D. B. (1969). Maintenance of children's behavior by accidental schedules of reinforcement. *Journal of Experimental Child Psychology, 8*, 222-233.

Winn, W. C., Allen, S. D., Janda, W. M., Koneman, E. W., Schreckenberger, P. C., Procop, G. W., & Woods, G. L. (2006). *Koneman's color atlas and textbook of diagnostic microbiology.* Philadelphia, PA: Lippincott Williams & Wilkins.

Young, E. (1998). *Cat and rat: The legend of the Chinese zodiac.* New York: Henry Holt and Co.

Zeeb, F. D., Robbins, T. W., & Winstanley, C. A. (2009). Serotonergic and dopaminergic modulation of gambling behavior as assessed using a novel rat gambling task. *Neuropsychopharmacology, 34*, 2329-2343.

Zilski-Pineño, J. M., & Pineño, O. (2007). Should we talk to the general public about our work? *International Journal of Comparative Psychology, 20*, 10-12.

INDEX

10927334R00126

Made in the USA
Charleston, SC
16 January 2012